OPTIMAL
NUTRITION
for OPTIMAL
HEALTH

OPTIMAL NUTRITION for OPTIMAL HEALTH

Thomas E. Levy, M.D., J.D.

Foreword by
Hal A. Huggins, D.D.S., M.S.

Keats Publishing

Chicago   New York   San Francisco   Lisbon   London   Madrid   Mexico City
Milan   New Delhi   San Juan   Seoul   Singapore   Sydney   Toronto

Library of Congress Cataloging-in-Publication Data

Levy, Thomas E.
    Optimal nutrition for optimal health : the real truth about eating
right for weight loss, detoxification, low cholesterol, better
digestion, and overall well-being / Thomas E. Levy ; foreword by Hal A.
Huggins
        p. cm.
    Includes bibliographical references and index.
    ISBN 0-658-01693-8 (alk. paper)
    1. Nutrition. 2. Detoxification (Health) I. Title.
  RA784 .L485 2001
  613.2--dc21

                                          2001037257

Keats Publishing

A Division of The **McGraw·Hill** *Companies*

1 2 3 4 5 6 7 8 9 0   DOC/DOC   0 9 8 7 6 5 4 3 2 1

ISBN 0-658-01693-8

This book was set in Palatino by Wendy Staroba Loreen
Printed and bound by R. R. Donnelley—Crawfordsville

Cover design by Mike Stromberg/The Great American Art Co.

McGraw-Hill books are available at special quantity discounts to use as premiums and
sales promotions, or for use in corporate training programs. For more information, please
write to the Director of Special Sales, Professional Publishing, McGraw-Hill, Two Penn
Plaza, New York, NY 10121-2298. Or contact your local bookstore.

This book is printed on acid-free paper.

To my beloved parents, Catherine and Isaac

CONTENTS

FOREWORD

Dear Tom,

Optimal Nutrition for Optimal Health is certainly not another dietary fling. If that is what readers are looking for, they should look elsewhere. This book is for people who want to know "why." When you know the "why" behind nutrition, the real problems become more evident. Overweight and underweight are not the problems. It is what the body does with the food we eat that we need to understand.

Tom, what separates you from most human beings is your ability to look at the various parts of a topic, make logical sense of each part, and locate what is really essential. The two most important aspects of nutrition—chewing your food and drinking water—are things we learn very early in life, and therefore we have little respect for them. You allow us to know "why" and provide us with new reason for looking at the complete picture. The complete picture is different from the whole picture. We can all look at the whole picture and miss most of the detail. When we look at the complete picture, we learn to recognize each component and learn where it fits into the whole.

Your interesting little trip down the intestinal tract impresses upon us the fact that the intestine is not a superhighway but a series of organs, each totally dedicated to one job, as if that were the only job in the world. But, as usual, you reassemble the body at the end, to show us that all systems have a common goal.

Folks, you will not get to know the real Tom in this book, for he is being very scientific and only occasionally biased. Controversial, yes—but that's because his experience may differ from that of people who have not traveled outside the four walls. I picture him typing with his left hand and saluting with his right hand.

I'm glad you exposed the rusty-nail method of iron fortification in cereals, Tom. Some of us are ready for that information, and ready to wander away from the herd action that industry would like us to adopt.

Such a different definition for the word *supplement.* A supplement should provide what is *lacking.* Boy, what a controversial concept! Most supplement sales are based on the idea that if a little bit is good, megadoses are wonderful. Diseases are hard enough to overcome, but with overdoses of supplements, especially the ones that are most heavily advertised, disease treatment becomes a confrontation with two enemies—the patient's lifestyle and the disease itself. Nutrition based on something other than TV ads can overcome both to a substantial degree. We just seldom give our body a chance to do what it is designed to do: Body, heal thyself.

Does Tom practice what he preaches? Well, for the most part, like most of us with passions, yes for 90 percent of the time. Then there are the tortuous human interludes. At a buffet recently, Tom looked at me and commented, "Don't let it be said I don't eat my vegetables." Then I watched as he picked up a piece of carrot cake.

Hal A. Huggins, D.D.S., M.S.
Colorado Springs, Colorado

ACKNOWLEDGMENTS

I have dedicated this book to both my mother and my father. They remain the two people to whom I give the most credit for my efforts in this book, and for the person I am today. My mother always provided delicious home-cooked meals, and my body never wanted for good nutrition while I was growing up. Furthermore, both my father and my mother always engaged me intellectually, and they both encouraged me to think independently as much as possible. Finally, they always loved me and always made it clear that that love would always be there. A better environment in which to grow up would have been hard to find.

My brother, John, and my sister, Cathy, have always been there for me as well. Even though John became a psychologist and Cathy became an engineer, they both always provided a reliable sounding board for me to express my latest medical or scientific thoughts, giving me invaluable feedback. John played a major role in opening up my mind to ideas that my traditional medical training tended to immediately reject, even though the ideas often proved to be true. And like my parents' love, the love I have received from both of them has been a source of great support and strength to me.

My brother-in-law, Tommy, and my sister-in-law, Delia, have come to be sources of great support to me as well. Having their love and understanding along with that of my sister and brother has only made my life better as I have grown older.

My good friend and mentor, Hal Huggins, has helped me enormously. It was he who introduced to me the incredible world of medicine *beyond* what I had learned in medical school, and beyond what I learned later when I served on the Tulane medical faculty, followed by the private practice of cardiology. What is even more amazing to me is that it took a dentist to teach me to appreciate the most important concepts of medicine. I regard Hal as having initiated my second medical education. His friendship and support have been invaluable over the past eight years.

Two other friends, Robert Kulacz and Lina Garcia, have also been very supportive of me and my work over the past few years. Both have been good sounding boards for my ideas.

David Groner has been a very good friend for a very long time, and his support has been invaluable to me for many years now.

J. W. McGinnis has also been a source of support and encouragement over the past eight years. He was president of the International Tesla Society when I first met him. Talking at the annual meetings of the society allowed me to expand my medical and scientific horizons—and it was at one of those meetings that I had the opportunity to meet Hal Huggins. J. W.'s friendship has been equally invaluable over the years.

Few have been as blessed as I.

INTRODUCTION

So why another "diet book"? Does the world really need one? Aren't there enough diet books out there already to thoroughly confuse the motivated individual seeking optimal nutrition? Certainly, in sheer numbers, diet books are among the most common of books today. And, yes, in spite of the amount of information available, getting scientifically accurate information on optimal nutrition is a most confusing and difficult task for most seekers. It is precisely *because* there are so many diet books out there that this book has been written. Most diet books contain a handful of good facts and a lot of self-serving fiction relating to the authors' personal experiences and preferences. Very few such books even attempt to be true to the physiological realities of how the human body works. This book describes the most important aspects of nutrition for maintaining (or regaining) a healthy body, including the natural reduction of excess fat.

In fact, this book is not intended to be another "diet book." Rather, it became apparent over time that the foods and nutrients that made sick people clinically better and less toxic also helped these people to normalize their body weights. Obese individuals would lose weight, and abnormally thin individuals would tend to gain some weight. The subtleties of just how food is digested and processed in the digestive system in the attainment of optimal nutrition also appeared to be directly related to how effectively fat was deposited into or mobilized from the body's tissues. Losing weight is the natural outgrowth of optimal nutrition. Similarly, eating habits that support optimal nutrition result in better absorption of nutrients and weight gain in those who are underweight. When you eat properly and digest properly, you need not count calories in order to achieve your proper body size. In fact, if you follow the principles of nutrition outlined in this book, you can achieve a healthy weight loss without ever having to feel hungry at all. To be sure, some foods will have to be completely avoided, but hunger will not have to be an additional burden.

Is everything in this book the gospel truth? That is certainly the intent. However, education and awareness are lifelong, evolving processes, and I continue to discover new facts every day. More importantly, I continue to discover new ways that both old and new facts can be integrated into both traditional and nontraditional ways of thinking scientifically. When armed with a unique enough perspective, even the scientific conclusions of "mainstream" medical and scientific researchers will often mesh well with many of the "radical" conclusions asserted in this book. Everything you read in this book will challenge you to think both logically and intuitively. As far as possible, every statement in this book is supported either by clear logic, by common sense, or by a source reference in the scientific literature. You are never asked just to believe my conclusions and follow my recommendations blindly. Rather, you are presented with the evidence and asked to reach your own conclusions. Only when you realize that nutrition is really a very scientific process that follows specific and fairly rigid laws of nature will you likely be motivated to follow the recommendations outlined in this book. And when you then begin to enjoy a healthier and less toxic life, you will be motivated to follow those recommendations as a permanent lifestyle. At the very least, you will have some important additional information to better understand why you might not be as healthy as you would like when you end up eventually ignoring or only minimally following some of the most important recommendations in this book.

Let me tell you what led me to write this book. Over the past seven years, I have had a unique opportunity to observe, question, and follow up a large number of individuals who have undergone what is termed a *Total Dental Revision*. This process usually involved the following:

1. replacement of mercury amalgam fillings with composite fillings tested to be as biocompatible as possible with the immune system,
2. replacement of crowns with more immunologically biocompatible materials,
3. proper extraction of root canal–treated teeth,
4. proper removal of dental implants,
5. proper cleaning of all jawbone cavitations, and
6. elimination of the infective toxicity of periodontal disease.

These patients had come to the clinic of Hal A. Huggins, D.D.S., M.S., in Colorado Springs, Colorado. Typically, these patients were all significantly ill, with multiple sclerosis, Parkinson's disease, Lou Gehrig's disease, and Alzheimer's disease assuming a disproportionately large percentage. Nearly all had some degree of depression, fatigue, irritability, brain fog, or other seemingly "nonspecific" departure from good health. Typically, the ages of the patients ranged from the late thirties to the early forties.

It is my belief and that of Dr. Huggins that toxicity from dental infections and dental materials is the source of most of the toxic exposure that most people face on a daily basis. Most of the patients who came through the clinic would consistently show clinical and laboratory test improvements promptly after their two-week treatments had concluded. It was in this context, along with subsequent telephone follow-up, that I repeatedly witnessed what supported the clinical recovery of these patients, as well as what consistently compromised that recovery. Repeatedly, specific nutritional interventions would improve the clinical status of these patients. Just as repeatedly, especially when the patients felt they had recovered enough to start "sinning" again, specific nutritional choices would clinically crash their immune systems and sometimes return them to where they had started, or occasionally allow them to drop down to clinical states that were even worse than where they had started. Furthermore, the results of blood, hair, and urine testing repeatedly documented that specific laboratory abnormalities typically accompanied these crashes. And it was repeatedly observed that these laboratory abnormalities, if followed carefully enough, would nearly always precede the clinical crashes.

The consistent conclusion that I drew from all of these observations was that every individual's nutritional choices—and especially the choices of one who is sick—cause almost immediate changes in laboratory test results and clinical well-being. Good nutritional practices help, and poor nutritional practices hurt. Following the book that I coauthored with Dr. Huggins, *Uninformed Consent: The Hidden Dangers of Dental Care,* this book seemed to be the next natural step to take in attempting to guide the interested public in finding the best ways to live the healthiest possible lives by finding ways to cope more effectively with ever-increasing amounts of toxic exposure, much of which is largely unavoidable. Optimal nutrition, in combination with optimal supplementation, remains the single best way to deal with the presence of otherwise unavoidable toxicity in the body, regardless of its source.

Much of the information in this book, then, results from the direct and repeated observations that one food may improve blood chemistries and make a patient feel better, and another food may have just the opposite effect. The bottom line is that the recommendations in this book are not made on the basis of what I *want* to be true, but on the basis of what I have repeatedly *observed* to cause clinical improvement in a given patient, typically accompanied by consistent improvements in different laboratory tests. Few other authors of "diet books" have had the privilege of having their recommendations and conclusions so clearly tested and reconfirmed on an almost daily basis.

Many approaches to nutrition seem more to be systems of belief and passion than proper programs of eating and supplementation based on sound physiological principles. For example, one diet that has gained a very large following has been the one that advises different foods depending upon one's blood type. In my opinion, this concept cannot be supported scientifically, although the uniqueness and simplicity of the diet appears to make it very compelling. Simplicity sells, even if the concept involved is incorrect. Except for the individual who has a legitimate allergy to a food or a food component, everyone, regardless of their blood type, should achieve good nutrition when the principles in this book are followed.

The vast majority of the population eats based on ancestral patterns, cultural norms, family customs, and lifelong habits. There are definitely genetic reasons for the predisposition to obesity and illness, but shared patterns of poor nutrition are probably the most important factors for shared poor health among family members. You don't have to just accept that you will be overweight and die of a heart attack at a young age because that was your father's fate. When any family shares the same chronically poor nutritional practices, that family will typically share a similar body type and health profile.

Another concept that emerged from this wealth of clinical information was that toxins are probably the primary factors that initiate or worsen most illnesses today. Whether from a dental source or elsewhere, toxins of all varieties act as continuous stressors on the immune system. As long as the immune system withstands the challenge, clinical health is preserved. However, when the toxic challenges finally overwhelm the immune system, disease will inevitably result. Furthermore, such a disease will also tend to become rapidly entrenched and chronic, since the compromised immune system rarely gets an opportunity to favorably respond to the practice of optimal nutrition along with the removal of toxicity. Rather, such an immune system is usually asked to recover in the face of unchanged toxicity and chronically poor nutrition. This is why so many people who become sick between their late thirties and their early fifties never again become completely well. They may survive, but they never again prosper. Too many people, along with their physicians, think that having their symptoms suppressed with prescription drugs is the equivalent of actually being healthy.

Nutrition is the primary way for our bodies to neutralize or otherwise deal with whatever toxins we face on a daily basis. And if you don't deal well with your toxins, you will not feel well or be well. No machine runs well on poor fuel, and our bodies are no different.

At first, you may feel overwhelmed by the amount of information in this book. Much of it will direct you to do the exact *opposite* of what you may be doing now. Furthermore, this book discredits much of the traditional nutritional advice given by other health care providers and nutritionists—a fact that may be difficult for you to accept. However, don't feel that if you cannot follow all of the recommendations in this book, there is no point in following any of them. The detail is provided so that you can be completely informed, and so that any compromises you choose to make will be your own choices.

I wish you well in your pursuit of good health and normal body weight through optimal nutrition and the minimization of daily toxicity.

THE IMPORTANCE OF PROPER DIGESTION

GOOD NUTRITION IS MORE THAN HEALTHY FOOD CHOICES

One of the most important concepts in this book is that a quality diet alone is not enough to support good health. Certainly, it will be better for you than the typical American diet, filled with sugar and processed foods. But good food can support good health only when it is properly digested. Good food poorly digested is not desirable, and poor food well digested is also not desirable. In fact, poorly digested food—even good food—can actually further stress your body and compromise your immune system. Therefore, you should never equate good nutrition simply with a selection of good foods. You must always address the quality of your digestion as well.

The definition of nutrition in *Webster's Dictionary* reflects this important connection between diet and digestion. *Webster's* defines nutrition as the sum of the processes by which an animal or plant takes in and utilizes food substances. This definition includes the processes of assimilating food and converting it into tissue. To talk about nutrition without even mentioning the digestive processes of absorption, assimilation, and conversion is incomplete at best. As we shall see, advising people what to eat without educating them on how to properly digest that food can actually be harmful to their health. At the very least, such advice misleads well-motivated people into thinking that only choosing the right foods ends their personal responsibilities in their pursuit of optimal nourishment for their bodies.

Let's now take a practical tour of the digestive system, focusing on how different food components are processed.

THE MOUTH

The mouth controls what is probably the most important part of the digestive process: chewing. Chewing your food thoroughly is the single best way to promote good digestion. Since digestive enzymes act only on the surface of the food that is presented to them, the rate and completeness of digestion are directly related to the total surface area of food that is exposed to these digestive enzymes. Many animals can gulp their food with little or no chewing and suffer no ill effects. For example, a snake doesn't chew at all. However, these animals have enormously more potent digestive enzymes than we do. A human being's relatively weak digestive enzymes can never completely do the work that is left undone by poor chewing.

Depending upon the kind of food you are eating, proper chewing can mean taking twenty, thirty, forty, or even *more* chews per mouthful. Do not consider your chewing to be complete until whatever you are eating is in a smooth, semiliquid form. Don't swallow until your tongue can no longer detect any significant lumpiness.

It is very important to emphasize that the primary purpose of chewing is not just to break the food into pieces that are easily swallowed. Greater ease of swallowing is only a relatively incidental benefit of proper chewing. Good chewing, through complex reflex mechanisms, also stimulates the increased production of digestive enzymes further down the digestive tract, promoting more efficient processing of the food as it proceeds through the gut. For this reason, silly as it may seem, you should even "chew" liquids other than water a few times to initiate these reflex mechanisms.

Likewise, foods that "require" little or no chewing should be chewed thoroughly nonetheless. Eggs are an excellent example. Most people can (and do!) swallow a mouthful of scrambled eggs with very few chews. However, a large clump of unchewed egg in the stomach can often end up incompletely digested. Protein of any kind is especially prone to incomplete processing when too little of its surface area is exposed to the stomach's digestive acids. One of the most common food allergies is an allergy to eggs, and the ease with which eggs can be swallowed without being well chewed probably accounts for this. The less completely a food is digested, the more likely it is that one will develop an allergy to that food or to a component of that food.

As the mouth initiates the digestive process with chewing, the salivary glands secrete saliva to wet down the food. This wetting, aided by the mucus content in the saliva, allows the food to be compacted into a mass that is more easily swallowed. The saliva also contains an enzyme called ptyalin, or salivary amylase. Ptyalin works to begin the breakdown of starches and other large carbohydrate molecules into simpler sugars. The acidity status of the saliva, which is typically neutral to very weakly acidic, allows the optimal activation of ptyalin. When any strongly acidic food is mixed with a starch, this initial breakdown of the starch is inhibited, because the ptyalin remains largely inactive.

Similarly, fat breakdown can be initiated in the mouth, as the saliva also contains small amounts of a fat-metabolizing enzyme known as lingual lipase. As this enzyme is stable in an acid environment, it can act after reaching the stomach's acids. The function of this lingual lipase is of greatest importance in the initial digestion of fats in an infant's diet. As a principle, it is important to realize that certain different enzymes cannot be active at the same points in the digestive tract, since one level of acid in the digestive environment can promote the activity of one enzyme while simultaneously suppressing the activity of another enzyme.

All enzymes in the body are sensitive to the level of acid in their immediate environment. However, some enzymes are activated by an acid environment, while others are suppressed by it. Similarly, some enzymes are activated by alkalinity, which is the opposite of acidity; or they are suppressed by it. This response to acid concentration, or pH, allows the body to exercise a sophisticated level of control over the point at which enzymes "turn on" or "turn off."

Chewing has yet another important benefit that is little realized. The longer you chew, the less food you will eat. Since most people seem concerned over their weight, this prolonged chewing habit is an important point since it results in a lower total consumption of calories. However, it is an important point for everybody, since larger meals will always be more likely than smaller meals to digest incompletely. This can lead to some degree of rotting and putrefaction, with significant resulting toxicity, as I shall explain in chapter 2.

The mind, through habit and reflex mechanisms, is often the primary trigger that prompts you to eat. This largely intellectual hunger is satisfied completely only by engaging in the process of eating for a long enough period of time. If you devour a large amount of food in five to ten minutes, as many people do, your mind may still crave more. However, if you take twenty to thirty minutes to eat that same amount of food, you will start to notice that second portions no longer seem so attractive. Remember: Few people really need to eat as much as they do. Short of real starvation, hunger is mostly a mental process, and the mind will not be satisfied if you stuff your face too fast, even if the caloric content of the food was substantial.

It is also important, especially to those readers desiring to lose weight, to realize that you shouldn't eat if you're not hungry. This might seem a silly point to make, but most people eat out of habit, and when lunchtime or dinnertime rolls around, they are going to eat something, regardless of how little hunger they may feel. The nutritional lifestyle outlined in this book will have the effect of reducing much of the hunger and many of the cravings for different foods that you may have now. In fact, most readers should be able to lose weight and strengthen their immune systems without having to deal with the unsatisfied pangs of real hunger at any time. Nothing could be sillier or more counterproductive to these health and weight goals than to proceed to eat when you are not even hungry. But many people do, and you need to be aware of this potential stumbling block at the outset. Be prepared to form a new habit: Don't eat unless you are genuinely hungry.

THE STOMACH

Once undergoing the critical step of being properly chewed, the semiliquefied food mass is squeezed down a muscular tube, the esophagus, to the stomach. The stomach is a far more sophisticated organ than most think. Rather than just being a passive sack for the groceries, the stomach plays a very active role in promoting proper digestion.

The human stomach actually has two successive functional compartments. The first portion of the stomach, the anterior part, has less muscle in the wall and will expand to allow a temporary storage of the food mass. The effects of stomach enzymes and acidity are less pronounced here, and the salivary ptyalin enzyme action can still remain active. However, before long, the food proceeds into the lower, posterior stomach, which is more muscular. The gastric juices, containing mucus, strong acid, and acid-activated protein-busting enzymes, then begin their work on the food mass.

However, this substantially occurs only if adequate protein is present in the food mass to reflexly stimulate the flow of the gastric juices. If starch alone is eaten, less of the acidic gastric juice will be reflexly released, and the starch digestion can proceed. More gastric juice produces a more strongly acid environment, which will shut down the activity of starch-busting enzymes that are present. Increasingly complex foods can present a wide range of protein content to the stomach. Virtually all foods contain at least minimal to trace amounts of protein, and the amount of acid formed in the stomach will be related to the absolute amount of protein presented to the stomach.

Lavers et al. determined that different foods of equal caloric value provoked vastly different acid secretion responses in the stomachs of dogs.[1] Relative to a beef meal standard, haddock resulted in 100 percent more acid secretion, chicken 20 percent more, vegetables 25 to 50 percent less, butter 60 percent less, and fruits 75 to 85 percent less. At rest, in the absence of any food, the stomach tends to be pH neutral, with only minimal, if any, acid present.

Another mechanism that helps to determine the acid content of the stomach relates to the acidity level of the food that was eaten. The more acidic the food eaten, the less acid the stomach will generate. A high-protein food will be less well digested in the stomach if it is eaten with a highly acidic food such as sauerkraut, since the stomach will reflexly form less acid as well as less protein-digesting enzymes in response to the presence of such an acidic food. You will see that this principle is very important in reaching complete digestion through the understanding of proper food combining, to be addressed in chapter 2.

In addition to exposing the food mass to the digestive enzymes of the stomach, the musculature in the lower, posterior stomach squeezes and churns the food, mixing it even further with the gastric acid and enzymes. This further promotes a greater meeting of the surface area of the food with the enzymes, which is directly related to how effective those enzymes can be in breaking down the food. In a sense, this active massage of the food helps to continue the "chewing" of the food after it leaves the mouth.

The primary digestive enzyme activated by the stomach acid is pepsin. Pepsin serves to break down proteins, which are long strings of amino acids linked together, into smaller amino acid sequences called peptides. These peptides, along with the rest of the digesting food, then await the next stage of the process. A strong muscular sphincter at the bottom of the stomach, the pylorus, prevents any premature release of the stomach contents.

Before proceeding to the next portion of the digestive pathway, the intestinal tract, it is also important to know a little about how the stomach empties. The pylorus at the bottom of the stomach serves not only to keep food from getting out of the stomach too prematurely, it also serves to let only a little of the digesting food, or chyme, into the intestinal tract at a time. Food does not just digest in the stomach for a while and then quickly get dumped out all at once. As the food gets progressively digested in the stomach, the pylorus senses this and lets a little at a time out of the stomach. Once the food mass has adequately liquefied and the food particles remaining have become small enough, the pylorus will start squirting no more than a teaspoon of chyme every thirty seconds or so out of the stomach. You will see why this is important after you understand some of the food combining principles discussed in chapter 2.

THE INTESTINAL TRACT

The small intestine is made up of three distinct portions. In sequence, they are the duodenum, the jejunum, and the ileum. The duodenum is the first segment to receive the food mass through the pylorus after its processing in the stomach. You should note that the additional digestive factors in the duodenum are alkaline in nature, and the acid-dependent stomach enzymes are typically shut down as soon as they are adequately mixed in with the alkaline duodenal environment. Defects in maintaining this alkaline environment can lead to duodenal ulcers, the most common form of ulcer disease, since the duodenum is ill equipped to deal with unneutralized stomach acids.

The duodenum receives important digestive factors from the pancreas, the liver, and the gallbladder, all of which are activated in an alkaline environment. The pancreatic enzymes serve to break down the protein-derived peptides into amino acids, the carbohydrates and starches into simpler sugar chains, and the lipids into fatty acids and glycerol. The bile from the liver and gallbladder coats the water-insoluble lipids, which enables the pancreatic enzymes to attack them and break them down. This process is known as emulsification, which essentially serves a detergent function, allowing water-insoluble substances to be processed in a water-based environment.

The lining of the duodenum begins the primary absorption of the broken-down food components. However, the jejunum, the next portion of the small intestine, completes most of this absorptive process. The lining of the jejunum, which is composed of numerous microscopic fingerlike projections containing even more enzymes, also serves to help complete the final breakdown of carbohydrates and peptides to single sugar molecules and amino acids before absorbing them into the bloodstream. Vitamin absorption also takes place here. The fatty lipids in the diet are critical in promoting the absorption of the fat-soluble vitamins (A, D, E, and K).

The final portion of the small intestine, the ileum, completes most of the nutrient absorption that is to take place. Much of the bile gets reabsorbed here, effectively recycling it for later use.

From the ileum, the food mass passes into the colon, or large intestine. The colon absorbs few nutrients, but it reabsorbs most of the water and electrolytes in the processed food mass, which is then delivered to the rectum for subsequent elimination.

WHERE THE NUTRIENTS GO

The intestine has a separate blood circulation that receives the absorbed nutrients. This system is called the portal venous system, which sees that the initial food product absorption is channeled through the liver. The liver then processes the nutrients into acceptable forms for distribution and uptake throughout the body. The liver also serves an important role in removing or otherwise inactivating toxic products to prevent them from being absorbed into the bloodstream along with the nutrients. However, a consistently poor diet or one that is poorly digested can overwhelm these defense mechanisms. The compensatory abilities of the body can only protect so much.

SOME CLOSING NOTES

The reader may well be asking why all this detail on digestion has any importance at all in the practical achievement of optimal nutrition. After all, if you eat something and you have no intestinal diseases, the body will do the rest, right?

Life (and health) would be so much simpler if this were true. Ask yourself why you eat the way you do. If you are like most people, you eat for taste and out of habit. Who ever declared that a bowl of cornflakes with milk was the proper, if not ideal, way to begin the day? Probably your mother and the cereal-dairy arms of the food industry. Trouble is, only your mother was motivated by what she thought was best for you.

This is the first major revelation that must occur to the motivated reader. And it shouldn't be a surprise. The food industry cares about the food industry and the profits it can make. This is not to accuse the food industry of any deep, dark conspiracies. All of big business does whatever it can do to legally increase its bottom line. What you have to realize is that no big industry or business has your best interests in mind unless those interests coincidentally mesh nicely with what the industry goals were already. Therefore, one rule of thumb you should never forget is: Advertisements and business publications are not valid sources of scientific information. They could be, and rarely are, but they are never to be trusted as such. In fact, as you will see as these chapters unfold, many of the most common pieces of dietary advice are exactly the *opposite* of the scientific truth. Whoever first declared that "Milk is a natural" or "You never outgrow your need for milk" was only looking to sell milk. The truth is that the dairy industry has never outgrown its need for ever-larger profits. Science be damned. But I won't be picking on just the dairy industry. Much more of corporate America must take the blame for the daily poisoning taking place in the name of nutrition.

Regardless of whether you are concerned about why you eat the way you do, you must understand that the way you eat must be altered if you expect to obtain the benefits touted in this book. Food can be tasty, and all of the palate's desires can be satisfied, but be resolved that many of the usual ways in which you've satisfied these longings in the past simply must be abandoned. However, and this is very important, do not feel that you must do everything that I suggest. Obviously, I feel that following all of the suggestions made would be optimal for your health. But much of what I'll suggest might be very inconvenient or even overly expensive for you to incorporate into your lifestyle. That is not a reason to avoid following any of the suggestions. Just about any of the suggestions can make their own small contribution to your pursuit of optimal nutrition. So, do what you can. You may well find that making one small change at a time will get you much further than trying to do everything at once and becoming overwhelmed and frustrated in the process, while rationalizing that life wasn't designed to be that difficult, and that you have to die sometime, anyway.

Although the end of the book will contain a listing of many practical and important suggestions for achieving optimal nutrition, I would also advise you to dog-ear pages, make notes, and highlight what you consider to be especially important points. This book is intended to make you a healthier person, not just to satisfy your intellectual curiosity and to answer questions that may have always had you puzzled.

FOOD COMBINING
PRINCIPLES

KEEP IT SIMPLE

In general, the larger and more complex your meals are, the greater the likelihood that they will impair your digestion to some degree. Animals in the wild rarely eat more than one type of food at a time. They may consume a variety of foods over time, but the foods will typically be eaten singly. Such wild animals tend to be healthy until their natural life span has run its course. On the other hand, our pet dogs and cats often get the "benefit" of human-inspired food combinations. Thus, as every veterinarian knows, our pets get the same degenerative diseases that their human owners get. Impairing your digestion might not sound like something that would be enormously harmful to your health, but we will soon see that it can really be just that. The body is something like a very finely tuned engine. The wrong fuel, delivered at the wrong rate, with other fuels or contaminants mixed in, will generally immediately impair the engine's performance and eventually just shut down the engine. The human body, however, can make an almost endless number of adjustments to food poorly digested short of the final insult, death. Rather than have the "intelligence" of an engine to sputter early on and eventually just not work, the body will plod along for an

extended time, coping with the toxins of poor digestion and ultimately acquiring any of a wide variety of chronic diseases. The
body will persist in staying alive and even be clinically "healthy"
for prolonged periods of time in the face of poor nutrition. Most
young people are still clinically healthy even though their nutritional habits are atrocious. However, as time passes and toxicity
persists, diseases will manifest themselves. Most people cannot appreciate how this is happening in their own lives, since most of the
world's developed countries are all in the same boat. Until there is
a sizable control population of people who are all eating and digesting correctly, and as a consequence are living long, healthy
lives, there will never be a wide appreciation by the public or their
health care providers of how sick they are making and keeping
themselves with their poor nutritional habits. And just because they
ate a certain way and felt well when they were younger will be no
justification for continuing to eat that way when they are older and
have fought toxicity for a much longer time.

Simple, small meals are always best. Convenience and habit have
many of us continuing to consume one or two massive meals a day
rather than a greater number of small meals. Not only are large
meals going to be consistently more toxic by mechanisms to be discussed later, weight gain will also be consistently more pronounced
by eating all of one's daily caloric intake at one or two sittings rather
than spread out over several more sittings. Look again at the example nature provides us. Many wild animals spend most of their
waking time continuously eating (grazing) small amounts of food.
Such animals are never obese and rarely toxic. Slow, controlled intake of nutrients tends more to be utilized at the time of eating to
support the body's functions, while large amounts of food nearly always trigger the conversion of excess nutrients into stored forms,
seen primarily as the epidemic of obesity across the country today.
A blast from a blowtorch could easily kill you, but the same amount
of heat delivered over an extended period of time could instead be

a welcome support to your health. Rate of ingestion can be more crucial than the total amount ingested when looking at overall health and body size.

Toxic digestion can also promote weight gain. The leaky gut syndrome, to be discussed in greater detail later in this chapter, permits greater caloric absorption from the food ingested as well as the absorption of toxins and incompletely digested foods. People who are obese and more toxic tend to have more prolonged bowel transit times. Their food simply spends more time in the gut than it should. Constipation of varying degrees will promote this excess absorption of both toxins and caloric content. If you are not having at *least* one substantial bowel movement per day, you are constipated to some degree. Consider this: You cannot leave any fleshy food such as meat sitting out on your kitchen counter without refrigeration for more than a day before it begins to noticeably rot and stink. Since your intestinal tract is a vastly better environment for bacterial growth than your kitchen counter, it shouldn't surprise you that food trapped in your gut for more than twenty-four hours can reliably be expected to begin rotting to some degree as well. Constipation is never desirable, but the severity of its negative effect on health remains little appreciated.

If constipation is one of your problems, be aware that the traditional methods of treating this condition are only very short-term, symptom-oriented approaches. An enema serves only to mechanically help clean out what has accumulated in the colon. Professional colonic therapies serve the same function, but tend to be more thorough in effect. Laxatives work in different ways, but most serve to soften the stool, increase its bulk, or directly irritate the colon into contracting more regularly. Some of these approaches may occasionally be useful to help "get you going" again, but it makes more sense to understand what caused the constipation in the first place.

Generally, waste will be slow to leave the colon and rectum if digested food is proceeding just as slowly "upstream" of the colon.

The caboose goes at the same speed as the locomotive. One of the primary reflex mechanisms causing the colon to empty is triggered by the appearance of more food residue leaving the small intestine and entering the first part of the colon. Therefore, anything that slows the digestive process anywhere in the gut can be expected to contribute to some degree of constipation. Poor food combinations increase transit time in the gut and slow down the whole digestive process, which in turn promotes the toxic state of constipation.

Always remember the concept of rate in the support of the body's health. Anything that is good for you can be made toxic by an excess rate of administration, usually along with an excess amount. No exceptions apply, although many things have much larger margins of safety than others. Some psychiatric patients have developed compulsions and obsessions with continuously drinking water to extreme excess. Under such circumstances, too much water ingested too rapidly can actually do harm by literally diluting out the blood sodium levels to the point of inducing seizures, but no rational person would use this as a reason to stop drinking water. Nevertheless, even this most essential substance for sustaining life and health can be overingested, resulting in some form of clinical toxicity. Remember that all foods, supplements, and medications can demonstrate some toxicity when taken in excess and/or at very rapid rates, even when lesser amounts and slower rates are unquestionably beneficial.

GENERAL PRINCIPLES

As was already discussed in the first chapter, different foods require different digestive enzymes to be active in order to be broken down and properly digested. One enzyme might require an alkaline environment to work and another might require an acidic environment. A neutral solution or environment will not allow the optimal activation of either an acid-dependent enzyme or an alkali-dependent enzyme. Whenever digestive contents tend toward neutrality, digestion must proceed as best it can, without much assistance from either the acid- or alkali-activated digestive enzymes. Of course, such digestion is significantly impaired, but does still proceed as best it can. There are enzymes of lesser importance that can still be active in a pH-neutral environment.

When digestion is impaired for whatever reason, actual rotting of food can coexist with the digestive process. The amount of this spoilage will generally relate to how completely the physiology of digestion was offended. If the concept of having rotting food sitting inside your digestive tract somehow conflicts with your common sense, remember that the entire digestive tract is filled with bacteria. While much of the bacterial population has important and beneficial effects in the proper processing of food when digestion is proceeding properly, the opposite can easily occur when proper digestion has been impaired. Anyone's digestive tract, given the opportunity, is an absolutely perfect environment to promote bacterial growth far beyond its desirable level. The inside of the gut is warm and wet. When bacteria and undigested food are added to this environment, you have an ideal culture medium for most common bacteria. The bowel movements of some people can make a bathroom unusable for an extended period of time, while the bowel movements of other people are almost free of any significant foul odor. This illustrates the difference between good and bad digestion.

Similarly, stomach contents do not have to be foul smelling, although many people think that is the case. There are enough occasions in the practice of medicine when there is the need to empty the stomach through a tube. Hospital workers can all tell you that stomach contents do not always smell poorly. However, when one gets sick enough to vomit, the contents are usually putrid and malodorous. The urge to vomit is often directly related to the ongoing rotting of the stomach contents after the normal digestive process had been inhibited or already spoiling food had been eaten. The stomach represents the last point at which the body can easily rid itself of rapidly rotting food. If the stomach lets its contents into the duodenum and beyond, diarrhea will be the only mechanical way to get rid of the increasingly toxic food mass, but not before the very absorptive small intestine admits significant toxins into the bloodstream.

It is precisely because of this relatively delicate balance between the proper digestion of foods and the potential rotting of those foods that food combining principles are so important. If you research these concepts further on your own, you will also find that food combining has its very vocal critics. Of course, every health recommendation has its supporters and critics. I would advise you to let your body be your guide. If, after combining your foods properly, you find that your gas, belching, bloating, heartburn, and flatulence are lessening (or even disappearing!) for the first time in memory, I doubt that you'll be very interested in giving much consideration to what the critics of food combining have to say.

Most of the concepts of food combining are supported by the most basic of scientific principles, as well as by common sense. The enzyme ptyalin in the saliva is most active when in a medium that is very close to neutral in pH. Most salivas are normally very close to this neutral pH, which allows the ptyalin to function. Ptyalin is an amylase that initiates the breakdown of carbohydrates and starches into simpler sugars. If not interrupted before reaching the intestinal amylases beyond the stomach, this carbohydrate breakdown can be up to 75 percent complete just from the effect of this initial amylase in the saliva.

What will reliably interrupt this process is a strongly acidic environment. When unstimulated without the active secretion of its own digestive enzymes, the stomach can also be close to pH neutrality in its resting state. In this case, a starch that began its processing in the mouth can continue its proper digestion even after arriving in the stomach. However, when protein—especially animal protein—is eaten at the same time, the stomach rapidly produces acid and acid-activated enzymes. When the starchy food from the mouth then completely mixes with these acidic stomach contents, the ptyalin from the mouth stops working. The starch and carbohydrate then have a greater opportunity to ferment (rather than digest normally) before their proper breakdown can resume in the duodenum and beyond.

Whenever any stage of the digestive process is kept from doing its job properly, the food cannot proceed to complete digestion. Just because the small intestine also has enzymes that can break down carbohydrate and starch doesn't mean it has an unlimited capacity to compensate for a lack of digestion being properly started in the mouth and continuing in the stomach. Also, the enzymes of the small intestine cannot aid in the digestion of food before the food reaches the small intestine. This means that any fermentation or rotting that begins in the stomach cannot be reversed or neutralized when the food finally reaches the small intestine. In short, only food that has not yet decayed can continue its proper digestion in the small intestine.

Another principle that further promotes this abnormal digestive fermentation is that carbohydrate and starch by themselves will usually pass through the stomach much more rapidly than when combined with a high-protein food. When forced to sit around in the stomach longer than necessary, bacteria rather than enzymes get a greater opportunity to feed and metabolize upon such food. Bacterial counts are normally suppressed by the stomach acid, but these counts will not stay low indefinitely when the starch is not allowed to leave the stomach fairly promptly. Such fermentation not only interrupts the proper digestion of starchy food into glucose and other simple sugars, it also causes these starches to be converted to toxic organic compounds. The substances that are commonly formed from the fermentation of starchy foods in the place of their proper digestion are acetic acid, alcohol, butyric acid, and lactic acid. To further worsen this process, the presence of any of these organic acids in the stomach will lessen the subsequent secretion of the gastric juice essential to the breakdown of any protein eaten. When the stomach already senses the presence of significant additional acidity, it naturally thinks less additional acid needs to be produced, resulting in a decreased release of acid from some of the stomach cells. And to make things worse, the stomach cells that release the essential digestive enzymes needed to break down the protein are inhibited in this release by this extra acid. This means that the presence of more abnormal acids in the stomach either from highly acidic foods or from the process of fermentation results in a smaller total amount of stomach enzymes available to help the digestion. High stomach acid content alone does not digest food.

Of course, there are enormous individual variations in much of human physiology, and the ability to withstand the digestive stresses noted above will vary widely among different people. However, even if you feel that you digest food perfectly well now without respecting these principles, you will still be doing yourself and your immune system a big favor by following them anyway. Youth and good genes can overcome a lot, but a lifetime of digestive stress will just cause any immune collapse occurring later in life to be more profound and difficult to reverse.

EAT FRUIT ALONE

An extremely important food combining principle is that fruit should always be eaten alone. When properly chewed, fruit will not usually be retained in the stomach for more than thirty to forty minutes (and often even for a lesser time). This processing time is far shorter than that of complex carbohydrates, proteins, or fats. Eaten alone, many carbohydrates will be held in the stomach for one and a half to two hours, proteins for two to four hours, and fats even a bit longer. Any food combined with fruit will slow the passage of that fruit through the stomach. The retained fruit will then inhibit the proper digestion of the other food, as that food needs more of the gastric juice that ends up being suppressed by the organic acid breakdown products of the retained fruit. This is essentially the same mechanism as with the digestion of the carbohydrates and starch, except that fruit needs much less processing in the stomach and so will begin to ferment more quickly.

If there are any fruits that have always given you indigestion in the past, try eating them first thing in the morning when your stomach is typically completely empty. Chew very well. You may be surprised at how well your body receives this meal. Many diets advise the limitation of fruit to one or two small portions a day. If you follow the rule to always eat fruit on an empty stomach, you may find that there needn't be such a limitation on fruit intake, unless you eat so much fruit that other important foods end up excluded due to a lack of hunger or appetite. Fruits are wonderful foods, and should not be minimized by nutritional counselors unaware of the manner required by fruit to be properly digested. Also, fruits should only be eaten raw, which further promotes digestion, since the natural enzyme content in the fruit hasn't been destroyed or severely limited by the cooking process, preserving process, or canning/packaging process. Processed fruits, especially those with added sugar, should be completely avoided. In general, the cooking of foods may be desirable in enhancing food taste, but many vital nutrients are lost in the process. The natural enzymes in raw fruit are also a factor in its rapid passage through the stomach, as more prolonged times are simply not necessary for proper processing and digestion.

COMPLEX FOODS

Complex foods containing both protein and carbohydrate in their natural state can vary in the completeness of digestion from one person to another. Many beans naturally combine significant percentages of both protein and carbohydrate, and many people do not comfortably digest them. Certainly, the guidelines in this chapter are not intended to have you ignore your body and the signals it might be giving you. If a food always gives you gas or indigestion, regardless of when or how well you process it, then avoid it. Not all foods naturally occurring in nature are well tolerated by everybody. Some people will actually have superior digestive abilities over others for a given food. For example, some people have the enzyme lactase that can directly break down the lactose in milk, but other people are completely deficient in this enzyme and intolerant to all milk and milk products. Genetically, we all have our own unique ancestral roots, and our digestive systems will typically digest the foods that our direct lineal ancestors ate better than other types of foods.

Critics of food combining like to point out that no foods are pure carbohydrate, pure protein, or pure fat. They point to foods such as some beans that have significant percentages of both protein and carbohydrate. In fact, almost every food contains SOME carbohydrate, protein, and fat. The intelligent combination of foods is based on what the *dominant* nutrient is in a given food. The dominant nutrient is the one that is greatest in quantity in that food. The greater the percentage of dominance, the more easily that food will be digested when it is eaten alone. If enough foods are eaten simultaneously, it becomes impossible for protein, fat, or carbohydrate to dominate, and the digestion will be impaired by the mechanisms that I have just described.

WHAT ABOUT SOY?

Soybeans can be especially tough to digest since they contain substantial amounts of protein, fat, and starch. A meal high in soybeans could be compared to a meal with three foods separately dominant in protein, fat, and carbohydrate. Foods with such codominant nutrients don't necessarily have to be completely avoided, but you should be aware of them, since they can sometimes cause persistently poor digestion. When all else fails in the pursuit of good digestion, you should then proceed to completely eliminate such foods from your diet.

Soybeans and soy products can also inhibit digestion by additional mechanisms. These foods are high in a substance called phytic acid. Phytic acid is an organic acid, and we have already noted how organic acids, such as those produced by fruit that ferments rather than digests, can impair production of digestive acid and enzymes by the stomach. Soybeans also contain enzyme inhibitors that directly block the ability of the gut to properly digest protein. Ordinary cooking does not eliminate either the phytic acid or the enzyme inhibitors of soybeans. Only well-fermented soy products such as tempeh and miso are significantly reduced in phytic acid and enzyme inhibitors. Unfortunately for the general health of the population, the fermented soy products are consumed in substantially smaller amounts than the non-fermented soy products such as tofu and bean curd.

The phytic acid contained in soybean products does even further damage to the nutritional status of the consumer. Several very important minerals, including calcium, magnesium, iron, and zinc, bind readily to phytic acid, which substantially lessens their effective absorption and utilization. Remember: It's not enough to eat mineral-rich foods if the body cannot effectively extract the mineral content from them. And remember that every meal you eat that does not deliver adequate vitamin and mineral content to you will result in your body "stealing" such needed nutrients from internal storage sites. When these storage sites eventually become severely depleted, disease processes can be expected to start, and existing diseases can be expected to worsen.

This concept of internal nutrient theft also applies to any food that has been substantially or totally depleted of vitamin and mineral nutrients. Examples of such foods include white flour, refined sugar, and polished white rice. Every time a depleted food is eaten in the place of a nutrient-rich food, some degree of this internal nutrient theft can be expected to occur. Your body can only borrow from these storage sites for a limited time before replenishment must take place to avoid sowing the seeds of disease.

FOOD COMBINATIONS: GOOD AND BAD

ONE AT A TIME

For the sake of accuracy, you should begin with the concept that foods eaten singly will always be best for optimal digestion. Needless to say, most people will not want to follow such a regimen, and it is not being proposed as the only way to enhance digestion. However, it is the manner in which your body can achieve its optimal digestion, and you should be aware of this. Furthermore, if your digestive system has never seemed to work right, you may want to consider such a strict regimen of single foods at first before declaring your efforts a failure. If you then see some success, you can later add reasonable combinations of food and see if you can tolerate them well without relapsing into poor digestion. We will also see that following such an initially strict regimen in combination with a minimization of daily toxin exposure, such as through the removal of dental toxicity, can resolve or make more manageable some of the worst and most chronic digestive disorders. Many people think they have done everything possible to get rid of yeast overgrowth (typically Candida) in their gut. However, until they have introduced their bodies to proper foods properly digested using proper food combining principles along with the removal of dental toxicity, they haven't yet addressed perhaps the most important factors underlying such a problem.

PROTEIN WITH FAT, CARBOHYDRATE WITH FAT

There are two basically optimal food combinations: protein with fat, and fat with starch or carbohydrate. A greater level of complexity can be addressed when one considers the acidity level of some foods and how they best combine, but that degree of detail will not be addressed here. Probably one of the worst (and most common) combinations is protein with starch. Yes, this means just about all sandwiches, unless your bread is surrounding only a vegetable or two. Why protein and starch is such a bad combination will be expanded upon a little later.

Simple sugars, as contrasted with the more complex carbohydrates, should not be combined with anything. Fruit must be a separate snack, and if you can't resist an occasional refined-sugar dessert, eat it on an empty stomach. This way only you suffer the ill effects of the refined sugar itself. When refined sugar is eaten with other foods, both the other foods and the sugar will be poorly digested. The end result is the formation of toxins and the increased absorption of caloric content, which help neither your health nor your weight.

VEGETABLES

A word about vegetables. In general, vegetables can be safely combined among themselves, but they should not be combined with dairy, fruits, or other sources of sugar. Most vegetables can be combined either with protein or with starch (but not with both at the same time!) without offending the digestion. However, foods that have a relatively higher starch content, such as potatoes, rice, pasta, and bread, should not be combined with protein.

If you are strongly motivated to follow the most detailed and strict food combining principles, I suggest that you read *The Complete Book of Food Combining: A New Approach to the Hay Diet and Healthy Eating,* by Jan and Inge Dries.[1] However, if you are more interested in simplifying the process, while still avoiding the significant disruption of digestion by violating the major principles of food combining, consider the following practical approach to this complex topic. Assign the following foods and food types the following number:

1. Starches and complex carbohydrates (not simple sugars)
2. Vegetables and fats (except for high starch-containing vegetables)
3. Protein (typically meat, seafood, and other non-vegetable sources of protein)
4. Fruit
5. High dairy content (e.g., milk, yogurt)

Now that you have categorized most of the foods, combine these foods according to the following protocol:

- Eat 1 with 2.
- Eat 2 with 3.
- Eat 4 by itself, and never sooner than two to four hours after a meal.
- Eat 5 by itself, and never sooner than two to four hours after a meal.
- Never eat 1 with 3.

In general, keep your meal size small, and don't eat more than 3 to 5 ounces of animal protein at a sitting, although your total amount of animal protein intake for the day can exceed this amount. If you do indulge in poor combinations, minimize their impact by keeping the amounts of one of them relatively small (for example, half a small potato with meat rather than an entire large potato). Sample menus based on these food combining principles can be found in chapter 10.

Always be aware of your own unique sensitivities. The longer you adhere to the basic principles of food combining, the more sensitive you will become to your own particular digestive weaknesses. Any combination that consistently causes any digestive upset or discomfort should be discontinued. Always remember that poor digestion is not normal. Proper food combining makes *any* indigestion the rare exception.

MEAT

An additional word about protein. Many books advise that some proteins, especially meat protein, simply cannot be completely digested. This is not true. What IS true is that meat protein is among the most difficult foods to completely digest, and any compromise of food combining principles, or of the other principles of good digestion, will easily result in incompletely digested meat protein. Such incomplete digestion will result in the rotting of that protein in the place of good digestion. If you don't break the rules on how to properly digest food, complete digestion of meat protein can be anticipated in most cases. However, problems may still arise if your digestive system has been ill and functioning poorly for a long enough period of time. Only when you are convinced that nothing seems to allow proper digestion of the meat protein you eat should you consider severely restricting or completely eliminating meat from your diet.

Both the popular press and some of the scientific literature have asserted that red meat is one of a number of factors causing colon cancer. This has always been used as one supposedly compelling argument in favor of a vegetarian diet. In fact, statistical studies have revealed that the vegetarianism of Seventh-Day Adventists is associated with a substantially lower incidence of colon cancer than the general population.[2] And in 1990, the *New England Journal of*

Medicine published a very large prospective study involving over 89,000 subjects, concluding that eating more red meat and animal fat resulted in a greater chance of colon cancer.[3]

Statistical studies can be very useful, but they can also be enormously misleading. Not infrequently, they lead to a conclusion that is actually the opposite of the truth. Consider the following: First of all, when meat eaters convert to vegetarianism, they typically do far more than just stop eating meat. Often, people who stop eating meat have been advised to do so by their health care providers to protect against heart disease and other degenerative diseases. Usually not only will they eliminate the meat, they will also eliminate most of the processed foods that comprise so much of the modern American diet. Any diet that severely restricts the consumption of processed foods and replaces them with a wide variety of fresh vegetables will usually make people healthier, even in the face of no meat in the diet. However, it is not uncommon to have studies group multiple undesirable dietary habits together and then conclude that the target of their disfavor, such as meat, must be the only significant offender. Slattery et al. concluded that a "Western" diet was linked to an increased colon cancer risk.[4] Such a diet was one high in red and processed meats, high in refined grains and sugars, and low in fresh fruits and vegetables. Any one of these factors could be a positive or a negative factor, and such a study does not begin to differentiate the conflicting factors. Nevertheless, these are often the types of studies from which researchers conclude what is or is not carcinogenic in the diet.

Furthermore, many converts to vegetarianism will also start exercising for the first time in their lives. Alarmed by their doctors' warnings, these new vegetarians will also often develop an interest in doing everything possible to promote their health for the first time in their lives, including drinking purified water and buying organic foods. Yet, just because they also gave up meat in these dramatically changed lifestyles, meat ends up getting blamed for all of the negative effects of the old lifestyles.

It is true that meat poorly digested will have toxic consequences on your health. If you chew it poorly, eat large amounts of it at a sitting, combine it poorly with other foods such as starch, or drown out your stomach's digestive capacities with large amounts of water or other liquids when eating it, you can expect a portion of it to rot and putrefy, with completely predictable toxic side effects. Two classic American meals will reliably impair complete digestion of the meat in them. The great American hamburger combines bread, usually white, with meat (starch + protein). The classic dinner of meat and potatoes also combines protein with a starch. This combination of starch with protein is an especially poor one. In their book on food combining, Grant and Joice[5] cite the work of Lionel J. Picton, who in 1931, wrote about indigestion promoted by starch, which he called amylaceous dyspepsia. In this article, Dr. Picton discussed some of the work of the famous Russian scientist, Dr. Ivan Pavlov. Dr. Pavlov found that minced meat fed to dogs took four hours to pass through the stomach. Bread by itself took about one and a half hours. But when these two foods were eaten together, the food would take eight or more hours to evacuate the stomach! When this poor food combination is combined with wolfing down the food in large chunks and with drinking large amounts of liquids, it is virtually impossible for digestion of the meat protein to proceed to completion. The meat then proceeds to do what it would do if left out anywhere else: It rots. And not only does the meat rot, the starch in the food ferments as it is held back in the stomach, transforming the nutritive sugar breakdown products into alcohol and a variety of organic acids, as I explained earlier. Remember that proper food combining principles not only directly aid the digestion of different foods, they also directly affect the retention times in the stomach and other areas of the gut, which further relates to whether a food will digest or spoil. When every meal spends four or more hours than it should in the stomach, everything else downstream slows down as well. Bowel transit times increase, and at least some degree of constipation, with the increased production and absorption of toxins in the colon, will result.

Conversely, good food combinations help ensure that any food that remains undigested doesn't get the chance to be retained in the gut and rot before getting eliminated. If you are having less than one bowel movement per twenty-four hours, your bowel transit time is too slow and is likely making a significant contribution to your daily toxin exposure. It is also important to remember at this point that if something is done improperly for a long enough period, it doesn't gradually and magically become the right thing to do. In a NOVA miniseries for television entitled "Ice Mummies," a 5,300-year-old frozen man was found to still have identifiable food in his stomach. The food was meat and an ancient form of wheat. But just because our ancestors were improperly combining meat and forms of bread many thousands of years ago doesn't mean that way of eating agrees with our digestive physiology any better now than it did then.

Although evolutionary considerations seem to allow one culture to digest certain types of foods chronically eaten throughout its ancestral history better than other foods, this form of adaptation should not be confused with the contradiction of basic physiological principles that have not significantly changed during man's traceable history. Man has been drinking a wide variety of alcoholic beverages for thousands of years, and man has been smoking tobacco and other combustibles for thousands of years. The test of time has not made these two culturally ingrained habits any less toxic and detrimental to our health than when they were done in ancient times.

When proteins putrefy, they are essentially allowing the bacteria in the gut to grow unchecked and out of balance, and a large number of by-products from this surge of bacterial metabolism ends up being produced. When food ends up trapped in various areas of the gut for a long enough period of time, as commonly occurs in a poorly functioning intestine, or even in the stomach, the conditions become ripe for the growth of bacteria that require little or no oxygen. These are called anaerobic bacteria. Multiplying anaerobic bacteria produce some of the most toxic substances ever discovered. One of the most chilling examples of this kind of toxicity is botulism. Botulism occurs when an anaerobic bacterium, *Clostridium botulinum*, gets trapped without oxygen, as might occur in a vacuum-packed can of food, for example. But botulism-like poisoning can also occur in a very chronic, low-grade fashion when a wide variety of anaerobic bacteria, including different *Clostridium* species, get the opportunity to multiply on undigested foods, especially meat protein.

Specific research on this subject by Maier et al. showed that the levels of these toxic anaerobic bacteria increased when the diet was high in red meat.[6] Conversely, meat-free diets resulted in aerobic (oxygen-requiring, less toxic) bacteria predominating. Of course, there is no indication that the principles of proper digestion and food combining were being followed by the students tested in this study when the meat was part of the diet. It should also be pointed out that much of the positive effect of a vegetarian diet probably relates directly to the combinations of foods typically eaten in a vegetarian diet. Specifically, the very lack of meat in such a diet makes many of the food combinations even taken by chance in a vegetarian diet acceptable ones. This proper combining will also consistently result in shorter bowel transit times, with more frequent bowel movements, usually several per day. A shortened bowel transit time is an enormously important factor in keeping down the populations of toxic bacteria in the gut. With relatively few exceptions, the only consistently poor combination that will commonly be seen on a vegetarian diet is the addition of fruits or dairy products to a vegetable meal. But it should also be remembered that this combination is still a very bad combination, and a few slices of fruit are a common part of a vegetarian meal. The resultant recommendation is that a large amount of vegetables along with a small amount of added meat, as long as the meat is properly digested, should represent the healthiest of all nutritional regimens.

The bacterial toxins from rotting food can have several negative effects on health. They can be directly absorbed by the intestine into the blood and lymphatic circulations. From there they can exert a toxic effect on virtually any part of the body. They can also have a direct toxic effect on the absorptive intestinal lining. The intestine is supposed to be selective in its absorption of properly broken-down foods. However, toxins can be one cause, perhaps a primary cause, of the "leaky gut" syndrome, which results in the intestine absorbing into the body much more than should be absorbed. This results in incompletely digested fragments or particles of food, especially protein, getting absorbed directly into the blood or lymphatics. The immune system is immediately challenged by such an absorption. The immune system perceives these incompletely digested food particles as an alien "nonfood" substance, much like a microbial invader against which the body needs protection. This results in the formation of antibodies and other immune responses to the perceived invasion. This is probably one of the primary reasons why food allergies develop initially and then persist. If poor dietary and digestive practices are never changed, then almost every meal presents poorly digested food anew to the gut. The intestinal lining never gets a break, and it simply cannot heal while continuing to be traumatized on a daily basis. It also means that even good food poorly digested can result in a further stress to an overworked immune system, rather than result in a supply of positive nutritional building blocks to support the immune system and give it a break.

The degree of toxicity of anaerobic bacterial toxins should also be emphasized. The neurotoxin that is manufactured by *Clostridium botulinum* is considered by modern science to be the most potent lethal substance known. It is at least 15,000 times more toxic than sarin, the organophosphate nerve agent used in the terrorist attack that took place in the Tokyo subway system in March 1995. As many as 565 people were reported to be hospitalized by that toxic attack, and 5 people were confirmed to have died from it. Even the tiniest amounts of such toxins should never be dismissed as insignificant.

So it is clear that meat can be very toxic to you if poorly digested. Is this a good reason to stop eating meat completely? Absolutely not. All foods can be toxic if they are allowed to ferment (carbohydrates), go rancid (fats), or putrefy (proteins) prior to proper and complete digestion. No one would dream of eating food that already smells and has obvious colonies of bacteria growing on it. But this doesn't mean that the food shouldn't be eaten if it is fresh. And it doesn't mean that any good food can't later become toxic if the principles of digestion outlined in this book end up being ignored. Meat has a great deal of nutritive value that simply cannot be matched by fruits and vegetables, in any combination. I address this subject at some length in chapter 5.

As emphasized earlier, the bowel transit time should be minimized and constipation of any degree avoided at all costs. Eliminating ingested toxins, following proper food combining principles, and taking adequate amounts of vitamin C as sodium ascorbate can all shorten the bowel transit time. Note that strong, chemical stimulant laxatives are not generally desirable, and they certainly should not be among the first measures taken to ease constipation.

OTHER INHIBITORS OF GOOD DIGESTION

In addition to food combining and proper chewing, there are other extremely important factors that play a part in optimizing digestion. Additional liquids should not be taken with any meal. The more liquid you drink, the more you dilute the enzymes that are doing the work of digestion. The potency of any enzyme is directly related to its concentration. Water, or just about any other liquid, will stop stomach digestion dead in its tracks when you swallow a large enough amount of it at mealtime. And as the digestion slows, the opportunity for food rotting increases.

Liquids can also impair digestion in other ways. Enzymatic activity is typically enhanced by heat, and impaired or stopped by cold. The glass of water served with your meal in a restaurant usually has ice in it. Double whammy. The enzymes get diluted and chilled into inactivity simultaneously.

Liquids can also be acidic or alkaline. Obviously, such liquids can directly affect the pH of the stomach contents above and beyond any dilution or chilling effect the liquid might have. Enzyme activity will decrease the further its environment gets from its optimal activating pH. And remember that any acid added to the stomach contents will further inhibit the stomach's release of its own acid, gastric juice, and gastric enzymes.

Liquids impair digestion by still another mechanism. The very presence of protein in the stomach further stimulates the secretion of acid and enzymes. However, this stimulation is related to the *concentration* of protein presented to the stomach. When significant liquids are ingested with the food and mixed up with it, the protein has a lesser concentration in the total food mass. With a lesser concentration, the signal to the stomach is weakened, and the continued secretion of gastric juice from the stomach cells is decreased. And without adequate amounts of activated enzymes from the gastric juice, protein in the stomach will simply not digest adequately.

Enzyme activity is also favorably promoted the better the stomach contents are mixed. Alcohol can inhibit the ability of the stomach to properly churn and mix its contents. An ice-cold beer with dinner can have a strong negative effect on stomach digestion, since it dilutes enzymes, chills enzymes, impairs mixing of the food mass, and decreases further reflex production of more acid and enzymes. Perhaps the belching that so often results from drinking beer during a meal is due as much to the digestion being inhibited as to the carbonation in the beer.

The amount of food eaten at a sitting will also directly affect the quality of digestion. The glands in the mouth, stomach, and small intestine are not unlimited in their abilities to form enzymes and other digestive factors. Not surprisingly, the body's digestive capabilities can be overwhelmed by the sheer volume of food, no matter how well chewed or otherwise prepared. This too can result in incomplete digestion. The amount of gastric juice and enzymes that can be produced in response to any meal can be overwhelmed by a large enough amount of food.

OTHER HEALTH PROBLEMS CAUSED BY POOR DIGESTION

By this time, you are probably a little queasy at the idea of having food rot in your gut rather than be properly digested. And you should be. Intuitively, you should realize that such a process is very toxic. As bacteria, especially anaerobic bacteria, multiply out of control in the gut, their metabolic products multiply as well. In people who have had digestive tracts out of whack for most of their lives, the toxicity of this process can be a primary reason for their poor general health.

Partially digested food on its way to becoming feces can become trapped in intestinal pockets. Such pockets can sometimes have little or no access to any oxygen. When these bacteria-filled pockets lose oxygen exposure, very toxic bacterial products can be produced. Furthermore, these pockets can become chronic and self-sustaining even after dietary and nutritional habits have been changed. Anecdotal evidence in individuals who have had chronically poor nutritional habits indicates that foods can sometimes be trapped in such pockets for years! Any disease process, left alone and neglected long enough, can persist even when the initial causative factors have been removed. Sometimes further measures beyond the mere removal of the initial causative factors must be undertaken. If you have made every change imaginable in your eating habits (including the removal of dental toxins) and you are still processing food poorly, you should consider undergoing a series of colonic therapies. However, a less invasive and possibly superior way to clean your intestinal tract and keep it clean is with large amounts of vitamin C orally (see chapter 8).

There is still another potentially severe consequence to rotting food and the leaky gut syndrome. The bacteria themselves, not just their toxic by-products, can also gain access to the body's blood and lymphatics. In addition to being an enormous ongoing challenge to the immune system, susceptible sites throughout the body can become seeded with these bacteria, which can then magnify their toxic abilities as they multiply inappropriately in these sites. Once this seeding takes place, the already compromised immune system often cannot clean up these sites. If the bacterial challenge is overwhelming enough to allow seeding to occur in the face of whatever immune resistance is present, a substantially stronger immune system will be required to do a proper cleanup. And this strengthening will never occur in the face of continued bacterial toxicity from incompletely digested food, or in the face of unaddressed dental toxins.

AUTOIMMUNE DISEASES

The seeding of these bacteria can also result in the initiation of autoimmune diseases in some people. Such diseases are characterized by the immune system attacking the native tissues of the body. Just as the poorly broken-down food particles can provoke an immune response, the bacteria themselves, along with their metabolic by-products, can also provoke the immune system into attacking normal body tissues. This happens when the immune system reacts against the body's own tissues that have been altered enough by the presence of the bacteria for the immune system to no longer recognize that tissue as being part of the body. The result is an auto-immune disease.

Gas

The bacteria in the gut can produce still another source of toxicity. In addition to the "solid" toxins produced on site by the bacterial metabolism, increases in bacteria count also result in the production of a large amount of intestinal gases. Under normal conditions, some gas production will result regardless of the food eaten and the state of the digestion. In fact, the amount of gas normally produced in or delivered to the colon ranges from 7 to 10 liters each day. However, the amount that gets passed through the anus is little more than a half liter. This is because over 90 percent of the gas formed in the digestive system is absorbed directly by the mucous lining of the intestine. Normally, this would not be a toxic process. However, when bacterial activity increases, especially with the emergence of the anaerobic forms mentioned earlier, the gases formed are toxic. Although the liver will help to detoxify the gas-absorbing blood that passes through the intestine, it will eventually become overwhelmed if the toxicity is not lessened through the proper digestion of good food.

One of the best-known intestinal gases is hydrogen sulfide (H_2S), known for its "rotten egg" smell. H_2S, characterized in *Dorland's Illustrated Medical Dictionary* as "an offensive and poisonous gas," is one of the gases that are formed when the undesirable bacteria begin to predominate, and its foul smell makes it one of the simplest and most easily detected indicators of poor digestion. However, few people realize that for whatever amount of foul-smelling gas they pass, almost ten times that amount gets absorbed into the body.

THE BENEFIT OF SPICES

Interestingly, one way in which you can probably decrease the sheer volume of pathogenic bacteria and other undesirable microorganisms in the gut is to increase your consumption of a wide variety of spices. Billing and Sherman published data suggesting that many different spices inhibit or kill a number of food-spoilage microorganisms.[7] Another study looked at the antimicrobial effects of twenty-four spices against a specific type of pathogenic *E. coli* bacteria.[8] In uncooked hamburger, it was found that clove had the highest inhibitory effect on bacterial growth, followed in potency by cinnamon, garlic, oregano, and sage. Interestingly, in a laboratory medium, garlic had the highest inhibitory effect. It was even demonstrated that increasing the amounts of clove and garlic could kill nearly all (99 percent) of the pathogenic *E. coli* bacteria without inhibiting normal bacterial fermentative processes. Garlic is often touted for its ability to promote good health. Perhaps one of its important mechanisms in accomplishing this is to lessen the amounts of toxins derived from the putrefaction of poorly digested meat and other protein. So, enhance both your digestion and your taste for good food with the liberal use of spices.

DIGESTION AND DENTAL TOXICITY

A number of different dental treatments have a toxic effect on the body, but the toxins themselves are either heavy metals or the products of anaerobic bacterial metabolism. Patients who underwent dental treatment at the clinic of Hal A. Huggins, D.D.S., M.S., commonly reported gastrointestinal symptoms. These patients came to Dr. Huggins in the hope that the removal of their mercury-containing dental amalgams, root canals, and cavitations would improve their health. In fact, in the patients who completed their dental treatment with Dr. Huggins, the effect of the treatment on the gastrointestinal symptoms was often dramatic. Bloating, belching, heartburn, and constipation often responded rapidly and significantly. Diarrhea, a symptom reported far less frequently than constipation, responded as well.

The conclusion Dr. Huggins reached from these clinical observations was that much of the mouth's toxicity actually dissolved in the saliva and was continuously swallowed around the clock. This was true both of the heavy-metal toxins and of the anaerobic bacterial toxins that were produced by root canal–treated teeth and other infected teeth. Both forms of toxins would be expected to aggravate the harmful effects that toxins locally produced in the intestine were already exerting.

Most of these patients had amalgam fillings in their mouths. These fillings appeared to be especially hard on the digestion. Amalgam fillings are generally a mixture of mercury, silver, copper, tin, and zinc. It is mercury especially that concerns us here. Although mercury is not the only toxic component of amalgam, it is the most toxic component. Indeed, mercury is the most toxic of the nonradioactive heavy metals. And mercury comprises roughly 50 percent of the amalgam mixture. Gay et al. and Svare et al. have demonstrated that amalgam fillings continuously release mercury inside the mouth as mercury vapor, the amount depending largely upon whether chewing is taking place and what type of food is being eaten.[9,10] Not only is mercury continuously inhaled in its vapor form, but it is also readily converted in the chemical environment of the mouth into inorganic salts and organic forms. Both of these, in addition to being absorbed into the body through the mucous membranes of the mouth, are also continuously swallowed in their dissolved forms in the saliva. This is a direct-delivery system of a very toxic heavy metal to the gut.

The mechanisms by which mercury impairs the digestion have not been clearly defined. However, mercury has been demonstrated to have some clearly definable effects on the bacteria in the gut.

Summers et al. showed that mercury released from amalgam fillings in primates resulted in an increase in both gut and mouth bacteria that were themselves resistant to the toxicity of mercury.[11] Remember that mercury is normally toxic to many bacteria, which is why mercury is used in so many topical antibacterial preparations. Mercury was also shown to cause the development of multiple antibiotic-resistant bacterial strains in those primates tested.

The bottom line is that this continuous exposure to the mercury from amalgam fillings causes a consistent and persistent change in the bacterial populations of the gut from the populations normally seen in the absence of ingested mercury. And the consistent clinical observation has been that symptoms of poor digestion reliably improve and often disappear completely after the amalgam has been removed. The patients treated with Total Dental Revisions were given many good nutritional instructions, but food combining was not emphasized. Adding the practice of proper food combining to the lifestyles of patients who receive Total Dental Revisions presents exciting clinical possibilities.

Although many of the patients seen by Dr. Huggins improved significantly after their dental revisions, not all did. Perhaps the minority who did not improve needed to adopt the other practices described in this book. It should be clear by now that very potent toxins can be formed on site in the gut in the course of poor digestion. The production of these toxins appears to be further promoted by the presence of mercury. However, some people can be chronically diseased enough that the mere removal of the dental sources of mercury might not be adequate to reverse the damage and restore clinically good digestion and good health.

FINAL NOTES

The way you eat and how you digest, then, are just as important as the quality of the food eaten. Don't be overwhelmed by all of this detail. There are simple, straightforward ways to choose good foods and digest them well. It's just very important that you understand as completely as possible why violating many or most of these principles of food combining and food choice (to be addressed) can be the primary reasons why you're sick, overweight, or both.

REFINED SUGAR: THE TOXIC TREAT

OVERVIEW

I could summarize this entire chapter in a few words: Don't eat sugar, it will kill you! Let's look at some very unsettling statistics. A little over a century ago, the average amount of sugar consumed per person per year in the United States was 10 pounds. By 1937, the amount had skyrocketed to 100 pounds. By 1958, this per capita consumption of sugar was up to 120 pounds. And now (fasten your seat belt), the average American consumes as much as 150 pounds of sugar per year! This amounts to well over a third of a pound of sugar per day. When you see what sugar does to your metabolism, you'll appreciate that it's amazing that the human body continues to live as long as it does (although it does so in the face of more and longer-term chronic degenerative diseases).

This tremendous increase in the consumption of refined sugar in the United States (and throughout the world) has been accompanied by an equally impressive increase in the incidence of heart disease-related deaths. Dying from heart disease around the turn of the century was relatively rare. Now it accounts for almost half of all deaths. Cause-and-effect, or irrelevant? The data strongly indict sugar as the primary culprit in this skyrocketing of heart disease, as well as other degenerative diseases, including cancer.

Sugar abuse can eventually lead to chronically elevated insulin levels in the blood, which will be discussed in detail later in this chapter. These elevated insulin levels not only promote the formation of fat in the body, they also directly correlate with the risk of heart attack. Pyorala et al. found that among healthy, nondiabetic policemen in Finland aged thirty-four to sixty-four years, those with the highest insulin levels were more than three times as likely to have a heart attack as those with the lowest insulin levels.[1] Since sugar abuse can be the cause of chronically elevated insulin levels, this suggests at least one mechanism by which sugar might be scientifically blamed for the skyrocketing incidence of heart disease today. Furthermore, overconsumption of sugar is one strong factor in the causation of diabetes, a disease that also increases the risk of heart attack. In fact, diabetes is such a major risk factor for heart disease that people with diabetes who have *no* sign of heart disease have the *same* risk of dying of a heart attack as nondiabetic people who have *already* suffered a heart attack.

Sugar abuse is also an important factor causing many people to be seriously overweight. Periodontitis, or gum disease, has also been shown to be independently associated with a greater incidence of heart disease. Saito et al. showed that obesity appears to increase the risk of having this kind of gum disease.[2] It would appear that at least one way in which sugar can affect the incidence of heart disease is in its ability to cause the obesity that is positively associated with the periodontitis.

SUGAR AND BLOOD CHEMISTRY

As a physician, if a therapy or medication makes a patient feel better, and if that patient's blood chemistries and other laboratory test results also improve, then I am comfortable that the right thing has been done. However, I do like to see the objectivity of such test results improving before definitively concluding that a given intervention was appropriate. Many people are so desperate to get better that they can actually rationalize that they are better. However, blood chemistries improve only when something positive has really happened inside the body. I certainly never disregard the importance of anybody's sense of well-being after an intervention, but I always feel the obligation to let them know if their physiology and general bodily function also seem to be improving. This is not to underestimate the power of the mind and its influence over the intangible pathways of energy flow in the body when people choose to treat themselves with nonmedical therapies or different forms of spiritual healing. Certainly, a positive mental attitude is felt by many to facilitate the healing process. Presumably, when such improved healing really takes place, there must be some associated improvement in some specific laboratory tests. Furthermore, if the improved healing represents a real, permanent change, the treatment or therapy that produced it must be able to withstand the ongoing scrutiny of long-term laboratory testing in the follow-up of the patient.

Melvin E. Page, D.D.S., found that ingested sugar had significant and consistent effects on certain blood chemistries.[3] Dr. Page found that proper nutrition could stabilize and even reverse many disease processes, in conjunction with minimal hormonal and supplemental therapies. He served as a mentor to Dr. Hal Huggins, whose work I described in chapter 2. Dr. Huggins took Dr. Page's work a big step forward by adding the removal of toxic dental materials to the nutritional regimen. The toxin removal appeared to accelerate the rate at which positive results were obtained in the patients.

Sugar consistently affects the serum levels of calcium, phosphorus, glucose, triglycerides, and cholesterol in a fairly direct manner. More indirectly, due to the negative impact sugar has on immune function, sugar ingestion will also affect the serum globulin levels, lymphocyte counts, and the liver enzyme levels to a limited degree. This negative effect that sugar has on immune function certainly helps to explain the increased incidence of endometrial cancer seen in obese diabetic women. Of course, obesity and diabetes are both sugar-related conditions. Shoff and Newcomb demonstrated that women who were both obese and diabetic were three times as likely to develop endometrial cancer as slim, nondiabetic women.[4] Sugar ingestion can have a negative effect on even a larger number of blood tests than those just mentioned, but these are among the tests affected that are most commonly reviewed by doctors.

Dr. Page found that his patients were healthiest when their calcium–phosphorus ratio was about 2.5 to 1. When this ratio was higher, as it would become upon the eating of sugar, he considered the body to be in a "degenerative" mode. This ratio has always strongly correlated with clinical health in patients followed after their dental toxicity had been addressed. Sugar ingestion, too rapid a rate of detoxification, or the exposure to new toxins would reliably foul up this very important ratio.

Dr. Page also made the very important observation that caffeine ingestion raises the sugar (glucose) level in the blood! For this reason, caffeine avoidance has to be given the same serious consideration as sugar avoidance. Even though some of the increase in blood sugar resulting from the caffeine ingestion is released from internal storage sites and not newly absorbed from the digestive system, the harmful effects of the sugar spike into the bloodstream will still be felt. And for those more concerned with weight than with health effects, caffeine can also serve to increase the appetite, and larger appetites are counterproductive to losing weight. Caffeine is so much more than just a stimulant that keeps you awake or makes you "hyper." But more about caffeine and its multiple effects a bit later.

SUGAR AND BIRTH DEFECTS

The concept that refined sugar in all its forms will make and keep you sick is not new. In 1989, Weston A. Price, D.D.S., compiled some very impressive data in his landmark book, *Nutrition and Physical Degeneration*.[5] Dr. Price traveled throughout the world, examining the lifestyles, nutritional habits, disease incidence, and dental status of numerous isolated tribes and populations of people. Even though the native diets would significantly vary from one culture to the next, Dr. Price consistently found excellent health and excellent dental hygiene among the natives who had not yet been exposed to the scourge of modern foods and modern food processing. Many of these people averaged less than one small cavity per mouth, even though young adults as well as children were examined.

Dr. Price also found that many of the infectious diseases that plague the modern world were skipping over many of these populations. Tuberculosis was especially rampant throughout the world at that time, but many of the cultures that Dr. Price studied were unaffected. Dr. Price then had the opportunity to witness what happened to these isolated people when the modern foods finally found their way to them. Specifically, refined sugar and white flour were the predominant "foods" that were introduced in a wide variety of forms. What Dr. Price then observed was as amazing as it was disturbing.

In the *first* generation of children born to mothers who were exposed to multiple sugar-laden foods, birth defects immediately appeared. The most readily apparent form of birth defect was deformity of the dental arch and the facial bony structures. Dr. Price noted that such children would have a general narrowing of their features, including their dental arches and the configuration of their noses. This narrowing of the dental arches resulted in crowding of the teeth. The physical configuration of the jawbones now made it impossible for teeth to properly appear and grow without a substantial crowding effect and the impairment of growth of other teeth. This birth defect caused by eating sugar and white flour resulted in the birth of a new field of dentistry: orthodontics. Modern parents now just accept the fact that their children will have to have braces early in their lives. They don't want their children to forever suffer the emotional burden of being afraid to smile and reveal a mouthful of unsightly, misaligned teeth. If only modern mothers really knew what to eat and what to avoid, at least during their pregnancies!

Interestingly, Dr. Price found that many of these "primitive" tribes of people would not allow young girls to be married until they had undergone a period of special feeding. Some tribes even required a full six months of special nutrition before marriage was allowed and childbearing could begin. These tribes knew the vital importance of proper nutrition in general, but especially in the pregnant female. They also knew that the body could not respond immediately, but needed to "build up" over a number of months to be optimally healthy for the duration of the pregnancy.

Dr. Price also found that sugar and white flour resulted in other developmental problems that were not as physically apparent as crowded teeth and narrowed facial features. He found that the immune systems were damaged by the ingestion of these products. The incidence of tuberculosis and other infectious diseases skyrocketed after the introduction of these foods. Dr. Price also noted the emergence of personality disorders among the populations that he studied. Mental function and acuity became compromised, and aggression appeared to develop to compensate for this decline in intelligence. Many of these tribes saw the onset of crime and other sorts of antisocial behaviors for the first time after the introduction of sugar and white flour. More "food for thought." Perhaps that's where that expression came from.

The importance of the proper diet in supporting brain function also gets support from studies done on the effects of breast-feeding on intellectual development. In general, it was found that the longer children had been breast-fed, the higher they scored on a variety of intellectual performance tests. Remember that the longer an infant is breast-fed, the less that infant will be ingesting the most common substitutes for breast milk: sugary fruit juices or formula-based milk sugars. This is a benefit above and beyond the enormous benefit of the support and stimulation given to the infant's immune system from the immune factor–rich colostrum, or "first milk" from the mother's breast. Not surprisingly, breast-feeding also appears to decrease the incidence of the common childhood illnesses. Wilson et al. published that breast-feeding and the late introduction of solids into the infant's diet may have a beneficial effect on both childhood health as well as subsequent adult disease.[6]

THE FORMATION OF FAT AND THE GLYCEMIC INDEX

The glycemic index helps explain the dynamics of weight gain and loss very well. Although it is not likely that this is the complete reason in all people why weight is gained in the face of substantial calorie restriction, it would appear to be a primary factor. But before going into what this index is and why it is vital in the management of one's diet, let's look first at how fat is formed, and how fat can later be broken down.

Insulin plays a major role in the storage of all the breakdown products of food that are absorbed into the bloodstream. Glucose (carbohydrates), triglycerides (fats), and amino acids (proteins) are all pushed into storage forms in the cells of the body by insulin. Obese people generally have higher insulin levels than people who are not obese, and any food they eat is more likely to proceed directly into storage as fat in the presence of this increased amount of insulin. This is one reason why obese people can eat very little and still not lose (or possibly even gain) weight.

Since the level of circulating insulin in the body is so important in causing food to become fat rather than to be directly utilized for energy, it is vital to understand what directly stimulates or suppresses the amounts of insulin released from the pancreas (the organ that forms and stores insulin). When glucose is released into the bloodstream from the digestion of food, insulin is immediately released to help metabolize that sugar. However, and this is crucial, the faster glucose is dumped into the bloodstream, the more insulin is released. The SAME total amount of glucose released more slowly over a longer time will result in much LESS of a total insulin release from the pancreas. Therefore, a "spike" of glucose released into the bloodstream effectively overstimulates the pancreas, resulting in an over-release of insulin for the actual amount of glucose absorbed. This mismatch of too much insulin for too little glucose has predictable and consistent negative effects on the body.

What does too rapid an insulin release do to the body? First, much of the rapidly released glucose that caused the increased insulin release will end up being directly stored as fat. And since this phenomenon is related more to the rate of glucose release than to the total amount of glucose being released, glucose can be stored as fat even when the total calorie count of the food is severely restricted! Any diet that restricts calories but still regularly allows for a sugary dessert as a portion of those calories totally misses this important point. If you want to lose weight, you must choose the right food and digest it properly. Delightfully, as we shall see, feeling hungry all of the time is not required in this weight loss process.

Also important in understanding this interplay of glucose and insulin is the fact that glucose, and not other forms of sugar, is the major stimulus for insulin secretion. Fructose, the major sugar in most fruits, has much less of an effect on the release of insulin. Fructose will affect glucose levels only after it undergoes a transformation process in the liver. Therefore, fructose cannot directly cause a spiking of glucose into the bloodstream from the gut with a corresponding over-release of insulin. However, when the levels of glucose are already high, both fructose and amino acids can help to stimulate the further release of significant amounts of insulin.

Obesity tends to become chronic and harder to fight when insulin levels remain elevated most of the time. Under such circumstances, little fat will ever be mobilized. Rather, circumstances then exist that favor just the formation of new fat and not the breakdown of old fat. Thus it is essential to know what causes chronically elevated levels of insulin to develop and to persist in the blood.

Here's where the situation can become enormously frustrating for the obese person. The cells in the body of the obese person, for reasons that remain unclear, become less responsive to the effects of insulin over time. Perhaps this represents a sort of "burnout" phenomenon of cells getting effectively torched over many years by large releases of insulin in response to spikes of glucose. Many medicines can become less effective over time as a tolerance develops to their effects. This would appear to be analogous to what is happening in the development of resistance to the effects of insulin.

And how does this insulin resistance affect the body? Simply, insulin resistance provokes the pancreas into making even *more* insulin until the job of the insulin has been completely done. When the regular dose of insulin doesn't do its job, the pancreas "perceives" that more insulin is needed.

And this is the metabolic profile of most obese people who are not diabetic: elevated insulin levels around the clock. In this state of chronic elevation, excess insulin is always present regardless of the size of the meal, and fat deposition can result from even the tiniest of portions.

What can be done to lower these chronically elevated insulin levels? This is where the great variety of responses will occur as similarly obese people follow the suggestions in this book. Like any other chronic disease, insulin resistance is not always completely reversible. But about 50 percent of the time, insulin resistance can be reduced or even eliminated by choosing the right foods and eating them properly. Clinically, this will mean that following the recommendations in this book will result in weight loss that ranges from dramatic to nonexistent. However, it won't do you any good to be overly pessimistic about what your response will be. At the very least, following the recommendations in this book will stop or minimize further weight gain. And it will definitely improve your general health, even if you don't achieve the body size that you want.

Mercury and Insulin

It is also of importance to realize that this 50 percent response rate of insulin-resistant patients doesn't take into account the profound effects of minimizing the levels of toxins being released into your body. For example, mercury (which is continuously released as vapor from dental amalgams, as I have explained) has its own effect on insulin metabolism. Mercury can directly attach itself to insulin, as well as to several other enzymes needed to process insulin properly. This directly decreases the effect of the insulin that has been released, causing the pancreas to release even more insulin to get the job done. Thus the presence of mercury can be one more factor keeping insulin levels high in the obese patient around the clock. Insulin-dependent diabetics must always guard against low blood sugar after they have had their amalgams removed, since the requirement for injected insulin often drops significantly after this removal. Continuing the same amount of insulin supplementation after amalgam removal can sometimes result in a dangerously low blood glucose level. It would appear that mercury from any source can worsen the clinical problem of insulin resistance that we are trying so hard to avoid. Therefore, it would seem likely that the removal of toxins such as mercury would allow significantly more than 50 percent of obese people to get a favorable decline in their elevated insulin levels from the suggestions being made.

At this point, it is also crucial to realize that any agent or factor that damages or lessens immune function will help mercury and other toxins to exert their toxic effects. Generally, the immune system acts to neutralize toxins, and anything that compromises the immune system magnifies the toxic effect. For this reason, immune system–damaging substances such as refined sugar can have a similar but less direct toxic effect on the body as mercury, since it allows whatever levels of mercury are present to be less neutralized and have a greater effect. This does not mean that sugar is as toxic as mercury. But it does mean that labeling a container of sugar with a skull and crossbones might not be overdoing it!

THE GLYCEMIC INDEX

Now let's readdress the glycemic index and how it is derived. The glycemic index was a term originally coined in the early 1980s, although researchers such as Dr. Page have long realized that certain foods release glucose into the blood more rapidly than other foods. This index has allowed a more scientific comparison of the glucose-releasing abilities of different foods. As we have already noted above, it is this rate of glucose release that correlates directly with the amount of insulin released, and with the amount of fat that is subsequently stored. Therefore, it follows that the immediate fat-forming potential of any food will be directly correlated with how rapidly it releases glucose into the bloodstream upon digestion.

The glycemic index is derived by checking blood glucose levels every fifteen minutes for three hours after the ingestion of 50 grams of the carbohydrate food being tested. This is then graphed out and the area on the graph underneath the curve formed by these blood values gives an objective figure on the rate of release and total amount of glucose released during the test time. These figures can then be compared among the different carbohydrate foods that are known to be digested down into glucose. Appendix I gives a glycemic index composite table for a number of common foods.

A NEGATIVE SIDE TO SOME NATURAL FOODS

Now for some shocking information. Some of the fastest glucose-releasing foods ever tested are potatoes, corn, white rice, and white flour–based foods, which would include pasta. These foods release glucose into the bloodstream substantially FASTER than sucrose (refined table sugar)! However, this should not be taken as an excuse to indulge in sugar, but to avoid these foods as absolutely as sugar if weight loss alone is desired. If you add to this the desire to achieve good health, refined sugar must be avoided in its entirety. However, this is not to say that the high glycemic index vegetables need to be as scrupulously avoided as sugar. Refined sugar has no inherent nutritional value beyond being a source of glucose. Indulging in refined sugar not only shoots up your blood glucose, it also suppresses hunger so that every indulgence in sugar keeps you from eating food that is genuinely nutritious. Certainly, potatoes, corn, and white rice do have positive nutritional value far beyond that of refined sugar candies and desserts. Such candies and desserts will undermine your immune system and compromise your nutrition no matter how little of them is eaten. Never confuse sugar's slightly lower place on the glycemic index as the equivalent of being more nutritious than potatoes, corn, and white rice. The index looks solely at the rate of glucose release into the blood and nothing else. It does not measure or rate the vitamin or mineral content of any food. There is probably no other commonly eaten food or food combination as completely lacking in vitamin and mineral content as refined sugar.

Remember that there does exist a wide variety of delicious and nutritious foods that will support your health and still allow you to lose weight as your blood glucose stays within a reasonable range. Few people intuitively would ever think that any vegetable or naturally grown food could possibly be less than good for you, but that is precisely the point, even though the numbers of them may not be large.

While it may offend some people's sensitivities to even suggest that foods such as corn or potatoes can effectively be bad for your health, you should consider what happens in your body every time you eat these foods. The surges of glucose into the bloodstream that result from eating these foods not only promote fat formation, they also sap immune strength. Further, these foods definitely promote and maintain weight gain, which ultimately has its own associated negative health effects. Remember that cattle are fed large amounts of corn so that they will get fat more quickly and produce the tastier fat-marbled cuts of meat. Animals (and people) are not fattened up by eating fat-containing foods. Sugar (glucose) overdose, NOT the eating of fat, produces fat in your body. All fatty foods and protein foods produce relatively minor changes in the blood glucose level after a meal. However, all foods can result in weight gain if you already have chronically elevated insulin levels, as discussed above. It's just that foods releasing glucose rapidly into the blood will always lay down fat faster and more effectively than foods that release glucose more slowly.

It's also no coincidence that corn, potatoes, white rice, and white flour are about the cheapest foods you can buy. Most people have limited money with which to buy good foods. Furthermore, most people consider these foods and the foods that are made from them to be among the tastiest and most enjoyable foods. French fries, baked potatoes, most breads, corn tortillas and tacos, most rices, most cereals—the list is very long. There aren't many meals—breakfast, lunch, or dinner—at which the average American family doesn't indulge in one or more of these foods or their derivatives. Believe me, there are MANY good foods out there that are not a torture to eat. But the recommendations in this book will involve breaking dietary habits that are as about culturally ingrained in you as are Little League baseball, an eight-hour workday, football in the fall, and baseball in the spring. In fact, the concept of "ethnic" heart disease has recently been introduced to the scientific literature. Winkleby et al. concluded that black and Mexican-American women have more risk factors for cardiovascular disease than white women.[7] In fact, women of lower socioeconomic status will reliably have the highest consumption of the highest glycemic index foods just mentioned. You won't find many low-income ladies having fresh (and expensive) asparagus as a side dish in the place of pasta, rice, or potatoes. It is doubtful that poorer women have some other unknown physiological risk factor for heart disease. Eating a diet filled with high glycemic index foods is explanation enough, as it will typically be associated with some degree of obesity.

Avoiding the very popular, high glycemic index foods shouldn't have you suffering with actual pangs of hunger in following the advice to avoid them, but you will have to deal with ignoring the appetites and desires for certain foods and food combinations that have been relentlessly hammered into you your entire life. Food is culture, and culture is food. You have to break those bonds, and your health and body size will then start to take care of themselves.

HUNGER

Some people reading this book might be impressed with all this information but are still wondering how they can deal with the seeming nonstop hunger that they have faced on every other eating plan they've tried. For most people, this will not be a problem. But first, appetite must be distinguished from hunger.

Hunger is the sensation of physical unease or discomfort that you experience when you haven't eaten in a while. Most people who have gone without food for twenty-four hours will experience this sensation. Prior to eating, they might even complain that they are "starving." There is actually a physical basis for this feeling. Severe hunger can be associated with powerful contractions of the stomach called hunger contractions. These contractions are greatly increased by a low level of blood sugar, and by the total absence of food. This sensation should not be a problem for you while following the guidelines in this book, even when you first start following them. No serious calorie restriction is recommended in this book, and most people will not have to worry so much about amounts as long as the other principles are followed. A significant amount of food can be eaten, although this concept should not be taken to unreasonable extremes. Seconds and thirds will not help you at all, and you should recall that too much food at a sitting is one factor that will reliably impair your digestion. Certainly, your weight loss would be helped by the addition of standard calorie restriction and regular exercise. However, the food types, the food combinations, when the food is eaten, and how the food is eaten remain the primary considerations for achieving success.

Appetite is entirely different from hunger. Appetite is a craving or a desire. You can have a craving or a desire for just about anything, but you should now realize that this is not the same thing as experiencing physical discomfort in your gut because you are truly physiologically hungry. Much of appetite is habit, and how motivated and determined you are will be an important determinant of whether you can give up (or seriously restrict) a given food or food combination. But an appetite can be eliminated. When you follow the rules, you will find that some lifelong cravings will seem to "magically" (and mercifully) disappear or lessen.

Why would any lifelong craving for a certain food suddenly change? You need to consider again what was said earlier about insulin levels. When a large amount of insulin is suddenly released in response to a large spike of glucose into the blood, another consequence in addition to fat formation from that glucose is that the insulin effect will "overshoot," and roughly two to three hours later, your blood glucose will be lower than normal, or hypoglycemic. This sudden decrease of fuel to the brain (which requires adequate amounts of glucose at *all* times to function properly) will prompt you to immediately eat more carbohydrate to restore that glucose level. In other words, you will crave any one of a number of different carbohydrate (sugar-producing) foods.

To prevent these cravings, you must avoid foods with a high glycemic index. Then your blood sugar will not yo-yo up and down, and many of these cravings, or appetites, will not be so bothersome, or will even cease to exist. Think about the foods that you crave the most. Most of them, no doubt, are high-carbohydrate foods. You may think you have a craving for a steak from time to time, but that craving won't be nearly as compelling as the craving that you have for something sweet in between your carbohydrate-based meals and snacks.

FURTHER SUGAR DAMAGE

Let's look at a pattern of eating shared by many, if not most, Americans today. The day starts around 7:00 A.M. with the great American breakfast: orange juice, a sugar-releasing refined cereal with more sugar added, milk, and coffee (usually sweetened with sugar). The glucose skyrockets and the insulin skyrockets in response. Around 10:00 A.M. the glucose has dropped precipitously low from the insulin overshoot provoked by breakfast. The resulting state of hypoglycemia now causes a feeling of sluggishness. Solution: the coffee break! Remember that even without added sugar, the caffeine hit releases sugar from internal stores and initiates another surge of insulin into the blood to metabolize it. Once the coffee break is over, there's generally enough sugar-stimulated energy to finish out the morning. Then, around noon, it's time for lunch. Since the overshoot of insulin at 10:00 A.M. again does not have enough glucose to metabolize, the carbohydrate craving sets in, and the great American burger or sandwich lunch is consumed. This has a doubly potent effect in producing sluggishness for the early afternoon. The protein portion diverts much of the blood supply to the digestion, and the bread (and coffee and dessert, if also consumed) once again has the insulin pouring into the bloodstream. Once again there is insulin overshoot, and you're praying for the afternoon coffee break to arrive so that you can stop and squirt more sugar into the blood to keep you going and give the insulin excess something upon which to work. You finally wake up from this new injection of glucose, and you survive until dinner. Dinner consists of another carbohydrate/protein disaster, but this time, when your glucose is dropping again several hours after the insulin overshoot response to dinner, you don't need to shock your body with another coffee break. Instead, you allow yourself to nod off to sleep in front of the TV. After a while, you wake up and go to bed.

But for many victims of this glucose-insulin seesaw, the torture does not end at bedtime. Many of these people also suffer from what is called the "night eating syndrome."[8] This was initially described in 1955. The foods consumed in this syndrome are typically carbohydrate-rich, and often the late night refrigerator raids comprise over 50 percent of the daily consumed calories! This is because the chronically high insulin levels induced by the glucose-insulin seesaw keep the carbohydrate cravings high. Often these cravings disrupt sleep and contribute to the insomnia of many who follow this routine. Insomnia may be more related to this type of eating than many health care professionals might suspect. Carbohydrate-rich foods facilitate increased serotonin production, and increased serotonin levels promote sleep. People afflicted by the night-eating syndrome can literally wake up to consume more of the foods that will put them back to sleep. And even if the disciple of this caffeine-sugar-carbohydrate routine does sleep well, the cycle repeats itself again the next day, and the bodywide glandular overload with eventual glandular burnout to be described next can proceed to develop.

With minor variations, most Americans subject their bodies to some degree of this glucose-insulin roller coaster on a daily basis. So what's the big deal? In addition to the chronic over-releases of insulin throughout the day that can eventually result in insulin resistance, obesity, and compromised immune function, the body, especially its glands, is being literally burned out. No one would gun an engine to its maximum speed every time it was started and expect it to outlast an engine that was properly warmed up and driven at moderate speeds with moderate acceleration. The body is no different. Rapid glucose release into the bloodstream can be likened to a metabolic blowtorch. The accelerator is being pushed to the floor.

What do these wide swings of insulin and glucose do to the body? In a word, aging. Any biological system that is chronically run faster than it is designed to run will wear down more quickly, be diseased longer, and die sooner. The pancreas, testes, ovaries, adrenals, thyroid, and pituitary are all glands whose functions are intimately interrelated. Other lesser known glands are also involved as well. When the body is subjected to wide swings of insulin and glucose, these glands burn out. Eventually, the body loses its ability to deal with environmental stresses, including toxicity, as well as with the poor nutrition that makes the toxicity worse.

These glands all produce hormones or hormonelike substances that make sure the body runs efficiently. Dr. Melvin Page found that administering relatively small amounts of hormones in conjunction with his dietary recommendations could turn around many of the chronic diseases still considered untreatable today. His patients' blood tests, as well as their senses of well-being, would consistently improve on his regimens, giving strong support to the validity of this reasoning.

One of the best examples of glandular overload and eventual glandular burnout is provided by the pancreas. When the pancreas has been overtaxed by wildly shifting glucose levels for a long enough period of time, insulin formation and release will become limited, and diabetes will result. While there are other reasons for the development of diabetes, pancreatic overstress is probably the most significant reason.

Corn has a high glycemic index. This is a primary reason why the Pima Indians in the southwestern United States have the highest incidence of diabetes in the world.[9] When modern, genetically engineered corn with large kernels and little fiber was substituted for much of the maize corn previously eaten by the Pimas, diabetes soared. Maize has a lower (but still relatively high) glycemic index compared to modern corn, but the more rapid release of glucose from the modern corn into the bodies of the Pimas was more than their metabolisms and pancreas glands could handle. To be sure, the Pimas would be even worse off if they washed all that corn down with soda pop and then had a candy bar. However, it is important to realize what an overdose of even a natural food such as corn can do to the metabolism. Even if you have no intention of giving up your favorite high glycemic index food, exerting some restraint and moderation can significantly lessen their negative impact.

SUGAR SUBSTITUTES

There are a few sweeteners available that pose significantly less risk to the health than refined sugar. There are also some that are quite toxic in their own right. However, nearly all sugar substitutes are harmful to some degree. None of them, with the exception of the nutritional supplement stevia, should be used without any restriction at all.

SACCHARIN

Saccharin (Sweet 'n Low) was discovered accidentally by a Johns Hopkins researcher who was trying to develop new food preservatives. Saccharin is a derivative of coal tar. Early on, saccharin was shown to be carcinogenic in test animals. Debate continues as to whether the high doses used in the animals are relevant, since humans consume much lower amounts. Even so, one popular brand of saccharin carries a warning that saccharin has been determined to cause cancer in laboratory animals. However, there are other sweetening alternatives available without this concern. Don't use saccharin products.

ASPARTAME

Aspartame (NutraSweet or Equal) is a combination of two amino acids, phenylalanine and aspartic acid. Remember that amino acids are generally beneficial only when a specific deficit is being supplemented or when proportionate amounts of all the amino acids are being ingested to promote the synthesis of new, properly balanced protein. Two amino acids, as in aspartame, that accumulate in the body in outrageously unbalanced amounts can eventually be toxic. Also, aspartame has a third component: methanol. Methanol, also called wood alcohol, makes up to 10 percent of the aspartame. Methanol's breakdown products include formaldehyde, which is a known carcinogen. Methanol is specifically toxic to the optic nerve, and has been known to cause blindness in a large enough dose. As of 1994, more than 75 percent of all nondrug complaints made to the Food and Drug Administration (FDA) were about aspartame. Avoid aspartame completely.

ACESULFAME K

Acesulfame K (Sunette or Sweet One) was FDA-approved in 1988. However, its chemical structure closely resembles that of saccharin, which, as I have just noted, is a potential carcinogen. Rats fed acesulfame K developed more tumors than rats not fed it. In addition, diabetic rats fed acesulfame K elevated their cholesterol levels. Avoid acesulfame K.

STEVIA

The FDA prohibits the labeling of stevia as a sweetener or flavor enhancer, but it does allow it to be labeled as a nutritional supplement. Canada, interestingly enough, takes the opposite approach, allowing stevia to be labeled as a sweetener but not as a nutritional supplement.

Stevioside, the refined form of stevia, is widely used outside the United States as a noncaloric sweetener. Forty percent of the commercial market for sweeteners is held by this substance in South America, China, Taiwan, Thailand, Korea, Malaysia, Indonesia, and Japan.

Traditionally, stevia has been used for flavor enhancement and sweetening, as an herbal tea, and as a medicine. Stevia used in its whole leaf form has been reported to have a blood sugar–*lowering* effect. Brazil has approved stevia tea for sale in the treatment of diabetes. Whole-leaf stevia has also been promoted outside the United States for a variety of beneficial effects on the cardiovascular system, the digestive system, the reproductive system, the incidence of dental cavities, the skin, and the control of microbial growth. Regardless of the weight one might give to such claims, stevia has been used continuously in Paraguay for over 1,500 years, and no report of ill effect has been made. And more currently, Japan has yet to report any ill effect from the use of stevioside as a sweetener despite heavy usage for over a decade. Use stevia regularly as a nutritional supplement, and any sweetening effect you get can just be a bonus.

BARLEY MALT SYRUP

Barley malt syrup comes from sprouted whole barley, which breaks down some of the carbohydrate into maltose. The syrup ends up being about 65 percent maltose and the rest complex carbohydrate.

Maltose has a glycemic index higher than that of pure glucose. Although some of the syrup is complex carbohydrate, the maltose content would promote wide glucose swings and hyperinsulinemia. Use sparingly.

Brown Rice Syrup

Brown rice syrup comes from sprouted barley and fermented brown rice. It contains roughly 50 percent maltose, and should generally be avoided or used sparingly for the same reasons as barley malt syrup.

Honey

Honey is a really mixed bag. When processed at all, it should be avoided like table sugar. After honey has been heated and strained, it loses much of the nutritive value for which it is touted. Some honeys even have other sweeteners, such as corn syrup, added to them!

Honey can also be a carrier of *Clostridium botulinum* spores. This situation is felt to be especially perilous for infants under one year of age, and honey should not be offered to them. However, no one really needs the seeds of such anaerobic bacterial metabolism in their gut, especially if that gut has been relatively cleared out by proper digestion and removal of dental toxins. If you indulge in honey, at least be aware of the dangers that it may pose. Furthermore, consume only honey that is as raw and unprocessed as possible. When pieces of the honeycomb are still present in the honey, this is one good sign that the honey has not been largely ruined.

On the positive side, honey probably supplies more vitamins, minerals, and trace elements than many other foods, and probably more than anything else used as a sweetener. Being in a food form, these additional elements are in a much more bioavailable form than if they were in a less-natural, supplemented form. Honey also contains enzymes that are of nutritional value, as well as proteins, carbohydrates, and a number of other factors that support the immune system and promote healing.

The best advice for the adult wanting to consume honey is to use moderation. Taken in balance with other foodstuffs, honey can be a positive health factor for most who consume it as long as it is free of processing. Royal jelly, propolis, and bee pollen are all derivative products of the beehive that likewise support good health, as they, too, contain a wide variety of bioavailable nutrients. However, people who are allergy-prone should always exert caution when first beginning the consumption of raw honey or any of the beehive-derived nutrient products.

MAPLE SYRUP

Maple syrup has about a 65 percent sucrose content. Although minimal vitamins and minerals can be found in this syrup, it is a poor way to get positive nutrients and a good way to get too much sucrose. Use maple syrup sparingly.

MOLASSES

Molasses is in much the same class as maple syrup, except that its sucrose content is usually slightly higher. Use sparingly.

BROWN SUGAR

Because it looks more natural, consumers often mistakenly believe that brown sugar is more nutritious than refined sugar or sucrose. This is not true. White sugar is 99 percent sucrose, and brown sugar is 96 percent sucrose. Brown sugar merely has a little molasses and/or caramel color added. Avoid brown sugar.

FRUCTOSE

Fructose is amazingly low on the glycemic index. As such, it doesn't have the overwhelmingly negative impact on glucose swings and insulin overproduction that most of the caloric sweeteners just mentioned above have. Crystalline fructose does not bring vitamins or minerals with it, but any sweetener will not typically be a source of good nutrients. With the exception of whole-leaf stevia and perhaps honey, your goal with all substances that have a sweetening effect will be to treat yourself to something that is only minimally harmful. Use fructose in moderation.

These are the best-known and most commonly used caloric and noncaloric sweeteners, and the foregoing analysis should help you to judge how much you are compromising your nutrition if you decide to use any one of them. Always try to satisfy your sweet tooth with the sweetness of a natural food, such as fruit. When this doesn't work, make an intelligent choice and do yourself the least possible harm as you indulge yourself.

CAFFEINE

Caffeine deserves a section of its own since it is so widely and extensively consumed while remaining very little understood. Beyond consideration as a stimulant that can wake you up or keep you awake, most people do not realize that caffeine has any other important effects. The very fact that caffeine can stimulate the body so strongly should send up at least a little warning flag that caffeine might not be so good for you. In fact, its stimulatory effect should send up a big warning flag.

Caffeine is being included in this chapter focusing on sugar because it works by releasing or mobilizing internal stores of sugar directly into the bloodstream, typically at a very fast rate. Therefore, all that was mentioned earlier about the negative effects of too rapid a release of glucose into the bloodstream applies when you ingest caffeine. And even though much of the glucose comes from internal stores rather than food just digested, caffeine nevertheless supports the maximal formation of fat from the sugar that was eaten, since it further increases the size of the glucose spike from the food with which the caffeine was ingested.

Caffeine, because of its glucose-mobilizing effects, is also a major player in causing chronically high levels of insulin. When caffeine is ingested in one form or another several times a day, it is very difficult for the insulin levels to dip down to normal for very long during the day, if at all. As already discussed, obesity is not likely to ever be reversed in the face of chronically high blood insulin levels.

What are the common sources of dietary caffeine? Coffee, tea, chocolate, sodas, and sport drinks top the list. But always read labels, since caffeine is a very popular stimulant, and any new food product could have it added. Although coffee typically leads the list for sheer amounts of caffeine delivered to the consumer, it is important to know that on an ounce-for-ounce basis, chocolate can deliver as much caffeine as some of the weaker coffees, such as instant. On the same equal amount basis, chocolate can deliver more caffeine than tea.

Chocolate can be harmful for a number of reasons. In addition to the caffeine content mentioned above, chocolate also contains smaller amounts of a related chemical, theobromine. Theobromine affects the body in much the same way as caffeine, but it is even more potent. When you take into consideration both the caffeine and theobromine content of chocolate, an indulgence in chocolate for some people could minimize the positive effects of much of this book's recommendations, especially with regard to weight loss. Chocolate can be a strong contributor to keeping elevated insulin levels up. At the very least, appreciate what chocolate is doing to you, and make it a "super treat" when you have it. Also, like all other sweets, eat it alone as a snack, and don't ruin the digestion of other good foods by eating them directly before or after the chocolate.

Most people realize how dependent on coffee and caffeine they have become only when they try to give it up. When one has experienced the headaches and general feeling of malaise associated with giving up caffeine, it certainly seems legitimate to consider caffeine an addictive substance. Small wonder that caffeine is added to so many popular drinks. Is there really any other logical reason for spiking so many soft drinks with caffeine? Even if the soft drink manufacturers say they want their products to give the drinker a "lift," which the sugar content will do anyway, the fact remains that children, who make up much of the market for soft drinks, are being groomed from a very early age to make the transition to the coffee rut as they get older. Of course, many adults just add the coffee to their routine, never giving up the soft drinks. The aging process then effectively accelerates even further.

Caffeine also tends to get glossed over as a very important substance for the pregnant woman to avoid. Not only does caffeine have all of the undesirable effects in the pregnant woman that it has in anyone else, it also can harm the fetus. Fernandes et al. studied the effects of moderate to heavy caffeine consumption during pregnancy and found a small but statistically significant increase in the risk for spontaneous abortion and low birthweight babies.[10]

Caffeine is a drug, and a pretty nasty one at that. Wake up to the real dangers of caffeine. It's not just for staying awake. Even if you can't get off of it, realize the dangers enough to help prevent your children from getting hooked and harming their health. The consequences will be paid if the caffeine gets ingested.

For those of you who are coffee drinkers who don't wish to quit, at least make every effort to drink properly decaffeinated coffee. Many coffees are decaffeinated by a process that uses toxic chemicals, such as methylene chloride or ethyl acetate. Try to find coffees that have been decaffeinated by the Swiss water process. This process uses only water to soak the unroasted beans, drawing out both caffeine and flavor. These beans are then discarded, and the water in which they were soaked is run through carbon filters, removing the caffeine but retaining much of the flavor. New beans are then soaked in this flavored but caffeine-free water. This new soak allows a withdrawal of caffeine from the new beans while removing much less flavor, since the water has already taken up flavor from the first batch of beans. This second batch of beans is then dried and roasted.

PARTING THOUGHTS

Refined sugar should be avoided as completely as possible in all of its forms. It is a major reason for obesity and compromised immune function today. And remember that decreased immune function will make any underlying disease processes worse and enable any underlying toxins or toxic processes to have maximal negative impact. Cardiovascular disease, as well as other degenerative diseases, are more a result of refined sugar consumption than any other single dietary component.

Similarly, but not as critically, high glycemic index foods should be avoided as completely as possible. A baked potato will never be as harmful to you as a candy bar and a soda pop, but it will make and keep you fat. If you are going to eat a high glycemic index carbohydrate, at least eat it as a single snack or food or with a vegetable, but don't compound the problem by botching up the digestion of good animal protein eaten with it.

Finally, if you have to have a refined sugar dessert or snack, eat it alone, and don't destroy the proper digestion of good food eaten at the same sitting.

MILK: A GOOD FOOD MADE TOXIC

ADVERTISING VERSUS SCIENCE

All industries advertise, but the dairy industry has been exceptionally effective in getting commercial slogans accepted as scientific fact. As we shall see, this trusting acceptance continues to have an enormously negative impact on the public health. Your favorite celebrity sporting a white mustache in an ad would be shocked if he or she really knew the toxic effects of pasteurized milk and many of its products. Sadly, most celebrity endorsers really think they're promoting a healthy nutrient to the public.

As this chapter unfolds, you will learn that milk is not always a bad food. Indeed, when man does not try to "improve" on the natural process of milk production, milk can go all the way from being frankly toxic to being enormously nutritious. Healthy milk comes from healthy cows grazing on fields with nutrient-rich soil. This requires the avoidance of continual growth hormone stimulation of these cows. This requires the use of proper sanitary processing techniques, without relying almost completely on antibiotics to keep the milk from being grossly contaminated. This requires the total avoidance of pasteurization and homogenization of the collected milk.

With all of these provisions, along with the existing legal mandates in America that all milk and dairy products be pasteurized, it's easy to see that owning your own cow would be the only way to make sure of getting healthy milk and milk products. The intervention of modern technology, with the support of the law, has made it effectively impossible for most of the population to ever drink a nutritious glass of milk. Because of these unavoidable realities, milk as it is presently available is far more toxic than it is nutritious. The technology of the modern dairy industry has been especially effective in negating most of the positive nutritious effects that can be gained from milk. As you will also see, there is a disturbingly large body of scientific evidence to support the assertion that milk is not the wonderful nutrient that the dairy industry would have you believe it is.

MILK AND HEART DISEASE

There are strong statistical links between heart disease and both milk carbohydrates and nonfat milk. Seely published these studies in the 1980s, but the science has yet to surpass the propaganda.[1–3] Interestingly, an especially strong statistical correlation emerges between heart disease and milk carbohydrates. Although a correlation cannot scientifically be considered the same as a cause-and-effect association, the data relating the increase in heart disease to increased sugar consumption (as noted in the last chapter) certainly suggest that the sugar in milk carbohydrates may be playing a similar role. Milk sugar, or lactose, is readily absorbed in the gut after being split into equal amounts of glucose, and another simple sugar, galactose. Further, the pasteurization process appears to allow a more rapid absorption of lactose, increasing the rate of glucose delivery into the system. Consistent with this observation, pasteurized milk promotes weight gain more effectively than unpasteurized milk. And heavier people end up with more heart disease than the lighter ones.

Being a ready source of sugar is only one potential mechanism for the increase in heart disease seen with increased milk consumption. We will also see that the pasteurization process itself can have negative effects on milk, and these effects can help to cause heart disease. Also, how homogenization and hormonal manipulation of today's milk and milk products all make their own deadly contributions to the final product will be described.

PASTEURIZATION

Pasteurization is the process of heating a liquid to a temperature high enough to destroy any microorganisms present that would otherwise eventually multiply enough to result in outright contamination, causing spoilage. In the case of milk, pasteurization is accomplished by one of three methods. The low-temperature holding method heats milk to about 145°F for thirty minutes. The high-temperature short-time method heats milk to about 161°F for at least fifteen seconds. The process of ultra-pasteurization heats milk to 280°F for at least two seconds. The temperature in this last method is well past the boiling point of water (212°F), a temperature that will irreversibly alter or denature protein and affect its nutritive value. All three pasteurization methods have significant destructive effects on the nutritive value of the milk.

The best practical demonstration of the negative health effects of this nutrient destruction was provided over fifty years ago in a study conducted by Francis Pottenger, M.D.[4] From 1932 to 1942, Dr. Pottenger examined the nutritive effects of raw versus cooked foods on the health of cats. As part of this study, he also examined the health effects of raw milk versus pasteurized milk versus two other types of processed milks. This part of the experiment demonstrated substantial negative effects not only on the initial test population of cats, but also on the next two generations of cats born to that initial population. All of the cats received as one-third of their diet raw meat and organs, as well as cod liver oil, to prevent too profound a depletion of nutrients in the test diet. However, the other two-thirds of the diet consisted of either raw milk, pasteurized milk, evaporated milk, or sweetened condensed milk. This divided the cats into a total of four different feeding groups. These different patterns of feeding were maintained through two more generations of cats.

Dr. Pottenger found that cats fed pasteurized milk as their principal dietary item developed skeletal abnormalities and lessened reproductive efficiency. He also noted that the offspring of these cats showed progressive constitutional and respiratory problems. In the cats fed the evaporated milk, the negative effects were more pronounced. And in those cats fed the sweetened condensed milk the negative effects were most pronounced. These cats developed much heavier fat deposits, showed substantial skeletal deformities, and demonstrated extreme irritability in their behavior. It would appear that the pasteurization process did its own substantial damage to the health of the cats, and the increasing amounts of sugar in the other milk preparations only worsened the damage initiated by the pasteurization. The bony abnormalities promoted by these milks in Dr. Pottenger's experiments are especially ironic findings since pasteurized milk is consistently promoted as being vital to the development of strong, healthy bones in people. For those wanting more detail, a full accounting of this work of Dr. Pottenger is available from the Price-Pottenger Nutrition Foundation in San Diego (see Appendix II). Many of the changes experienced by the cats and their offspring while on the different feeding schedules were even recorded on videotape, providing an even more graphic and dramatic accounting of how pasteurized milk with varying amounts of sugar can wreak havoc with the general health.

Pasteurization also profoundly affects the bioavailability of the calcium content of milk. In wholesome food, calcium is present in a bioavailable form that serves to strengthen bones and teeth, while supplying enough ionic, or dissolved, calcium to meet the normal metabolic needs of literally all the cells in the body. Calcium should NOT be depositing diffusely throughout the body in rocklike deposits. Yet this is exactly what happens in the habitual drinker of pasteurized milk. To make it worse, the added vitamin D that is routinely added to milk and so many of the other multivitamin preparations that milk drinkers take only further aids this abnormal deposition of calcium in the body's tissues. In fact, supplemental vitamin D can easily aggravate the dreaded calcium loss from bones, while increasing calcium absorption from the gut, both of which serve to provide greater amounts of calcium for this abnormal precipitation.

The bioavailability of the calcium in milk relies primarily on the integrity of unheated protein carriers found naturally in milk. The heat of pasteurization is enough to denature these proteins, meaning they have been physically altered enough by the "cooking" process of pasteurization to keep them from delivering calcium to the tissue sites where it is supposed to go. The three-dimensional configuration of these denatured proteins is completely changed by pasteurization, and the new configurations are just incapable of performing this vital calcium delivery function. But calcium is nevertheless absorbed, even though it is not properly delivered, and so it accumulates in the wrong places throughout the body.

What do these abnormal calcium accumulations do? Quite simply, they cause or facilitate virtually every degenerative disease known. The calcium deposits out in a rocklike form. The classic manifestation of this deposition occurs in the blood vessels, notably in the coronary (heart) arteries. The deposits either block these arteries or serve as a starting point for other artery-blocking substances to accumulate. When the artery blocks off completely, a heart attack is usually the result. This deposition of calcium in the coronary arteries represents another mechanism by which pasteurized milk promotes the increase in heart disease mentioned at the start of this chapter.

In following the hair analyses of many people who were treated at the clinic of Dr. Hal Huggins in Colorado Springs, abnormally elevated hair calcium levels consistently correlated with the drinking of milk and the taking of calcium supplements. Most of the patients under seventy years of age had elevated hair calcium levels. However, as a rule, the people over seventy years of age who came to the clinic almost always had normal or low calcium levels in the hair. The conclusion that seemed to make the most sense was that the "high-calcium" patients simply did not survive past seventy, due to the increased rate of heart disease, cancer, and other degenerative diseases facilitated by the chronic and excessive ingestion of nonbioavailable calcium.

This conclusion received unintentional support in the medical literature. Otto et al. published a study showing that aortic sclerosis, a condition in which the lining of the aorta (the main artery coming out of the heart) is rigidly inflexible and pipelike, is associated with a 50 percent greater chance of death from heart attack and heart-related causes.[5] In this condition, excessive deposits of calcium are present in the wall of the aorta. This gives some additional support to the concept that people with diffusely deposited calcium throughout their bodies just don't live as long as their noncalcified counterparts. In a review article, Doherty et al. seem mystified as to where the epidemic of calcified coronary arteries could be coming from.[6] In my opinion, the enormous consumption of milk, in combination with the widespread ingestion of calcium supplements (discussed further in chapter 8), accounts for this epidemic of body tissue calcification quite nicely.

BOVINE GROWTH HORMONE

Milk has long been promoted as a healthy, growth-promoting food. Certainly, in terms of physical size and stature, the ingestion of modernly processed milk and milk products is a strong stimulus to growth. But is bigger always better? Perhaps, but only if a long life is not one of your priorities.

In an interesting survey study on the effect of human size on longevity, researchers Samaras and Heigh found a consistent relationship. They discovered that longevity was associated with smaller stature or size, when not due to malnutrition, childhood disease, or prenatal disease.[7] Their study reviewed many other longevity studies, involving many thousands of subjects. While such an effect is unlikely attributable to only one factor, the larger people typically are being exposed to larger amounts of bovine growth hormone, both from natural sources and from the many injections of synthetic hormones currently administered to milk-producing cows.

In fact, the one thing that the vast majority of large and tall people appear to have in common is the frequent drinking of milk as a beverage while growing up. The correlation is striking. Conduct your own informal survey. See how many people you can find that are 6 feet 2 inches or taller, with parents 5 feet 10 inches or smaller (to minimize direct genetic contribution to size), who were not regular milk drinkers. You'll be hard pressed to find more than 10 percent of such people who have not consistently consumed substantial amounts of milk most of their lives.

Of course, most people consider this growth effect to be tremendously desirable. Hardly anyone wants to be short and small rather than tall and imposing, and nothing makes small parents prouder than seeing their children grow large and strong. However, the growth-stimulating effect of milk is an abnormal, unhealthy stimulation of growth in humans, not a normal one. The toxicity of the huge amounts of calcium ingested by the regular ingestion of milk as a beverage was just addressed in the previous section on pasteurization. Chapter 8, which addresses the concept of proper supplementation, also helps to explain why excess calcium, whether from milk or supplements, will often be attended by a shorter life span. You are certainly not "doomed" if you are already a tall, large person with many years of milk drinking under your belt. However, it would be wise to remove milk from your diet now so that your body can begin to mobilize the widespread deposition of calcium typically seen after years of milk drinking.

Recently a professional football player who had received recognition as the outstanding college offensive lineman in the nation in the early 1990s made a very interesting observation. He played at a weight of about 290 pounds, and he was physically larger than most of his peers throughout the country at that time. He noted that he felt like the small guy by today's standards. Today, less than a decade later, many offensive linemen weigh over 300 pounds, and a substantial number weigh 330 pounds or even more. Although some of these large players are grossly obese, many of them are not. Instead, they are just well-proportioned giants. It's hard not to conclude that the unrelenting hormonal attack on our commercial milk production isn't turning our nation into one large laboratory experiment. Androgenic steroids are also making a contribution to this emerging class of giants, but these drugs have been available now for decades and have not been steadily escalating their presence among athletes to the same degree as the bovine growth hormone in our modern milk and milk products.

Dr. Melvin Page, in *Your Body Is Your Best Doctor*, astutely noted that growth doubling rates varied widely among different species of animals.[8] These rates bear a direct relationship to both the amounts of growth hormone generated by these species as well as the degree of growth response to the growth hormone present. Dr. Page pointed out that a rabbit doubles its birth weight in 6 days, a dog in 9 days, a sheep in 14 days, a cow in 47 days, and a human infant in 187 days. By ingesting large amounts of cow's milk, our babies, children, and young adults are exposing themselves chronically to large amounts of a substance that allows the growing calf to double its size in less than one-third the time that a human infant should be doubling its weight. Ironically, many health care practitioners be-

lieve that people are larger now than they were decades ago because the overall quality of nutrition has improved. This entire book
provides the evidence to show how completely ridiculous that concept is.

You might be asking why extra growth hormone is being given to
cows these days. The simple answer is increased profitability. Cows
that are not injected with bovine growth hormone produce much
less milk. In the 1600s, before the dairy industry meddled in milk
production, a privately owned dairy cow would produce no more
than one quart of milk per day. By the mid-1800s, the same cow
would still produce less than two quarts per day. However, by 1960
the yield had increased to more than nine quarts per day. And today
some genetically and hormonally manipulated dairy cows produce
up to fifty quarts of milk per day!

Furthermore, the growth hormone contained in the milk is not
substantially affected by boiling, pasteurization, or cooking. Even
though the nutritive value of milk is strongly affected by such measures, the growth hormone remains largely untouched and fully capable of exerting its growth-stimulating effects. Not surprisingly,
then, the growth hormone is found in derivative milk products,
such as cheese. Heavy cream and butter, however, are largely spared
the presence of growth hormone, since they are animal fats that naturally separate out from the milk. The chemical properties of growth
hormone favor its concentration in the milk and not in the fat.

In fact, it has only been fairly recent that this enormous stimulation of our milk cows with bovine growth hormone has been ef-
fected, largely due to the official blessing of the Food and Drug
Administration (FDA) on November 5, 1993. Regardless of what the
FDA's true motives may have been, the paper written by two of its
employees, Judy Juskevich, Ph.D., and Greg Guyer, Ph.D., and published in *Science*,[9] along with the testimony of multiple other FDA
employees before Congress, resulted in the Monsanto Agricultural
Company being granted approval for the full-scale production of

rBST for use throughout the land. rBST is recombinant bovine somatotropin. BST is also known as BGH, or bovine growth hormone. Let's look at the first sentence of the abstract to the article of Juskevich and Guyer.

> Scientists in the Food and Drug Administration (FDA), after reviewing the scientific literature and evaluating studies conducted by pharmaceutical companies, have concluded that the use of recombinant bovine growth hormone (rbGH or rBST) in dairy cattle presents no increased health risk to consumers.

This comforting statement is later followed in the same abstract by the following assertion:

> Recombinant bGH treatment produces an increase in the concentration of insulin-like growth factor-1 (IGF-1) in cow's milk.

Robert Cohen, in his book *Milk: The Deadly Poison*,[10] effectively refutes eight of the major contentions in the review paper of Juskevich and Guyer, finding the opposite conclusion for all eight contentions to be appropriate. Cohen demonstrates convincingly that:

1. Bovine growth hormone IS biologically active in humans.
2. Bovine growth hormone is NOT routinely broken down in the stomach.
3. Bovine growth hormone DOES have definite activity when administered orally to rats.
4. Bovine growth hormone IS significantly increased in the milk of cows treated with rbGH (26 percent increase).
5. Bovine growth hormone is NOT significantly destroyed by pasteurization.
6. Bovine growth hormone DOES impact directly the nutritional quality of milk.

7. Bovine growth hormone DOES produce multiple other growth factors that survive the stomach acid and exert largely unresearched effects on the milk drinker.
8. Bovine growth hormone produces a growth factor (IGF-1) that IS orally active in laboratory rats.

Why go into all of this detail on the saga of how large amounts of growth hormone have ended up in virtually all of our commercially available milk and derivative milk products? The message of this book is not one that attempts to delve into the reasons why the government, the food industry, and the many involved researchers make the policy decisions, make the recommendations, and reach the experimental conclusions that they do. However, it can also be difficult to believe that the health of the population is not the overwhelming consideration in basic food research. The above information is presented to allow the motivated reader to research this issue even further; in the meantime, the information presented here can speak for itself.

HOMOGENIZATION AND XANTHINE OXIDASE

As we will see, homogenization is but one more step in the processing of milk that may further promote hardening of the arteries and heart disease. Homogenization is a process that breaks up the fat particles found primarily in the cream into such extremely tiny particles that the cream no longer floats on the top of the milk but remains distributed in suspension evenly throughout it. This process is designed primarily to make the final milk tastier due to the cream component and, presumably, more palatable to the milk consumer.

So what's the harm in homogenization? Cow's milk contains an enzyme of large molecular size called xanthine oxidase (XO). XO is normally attached to the fat globules in milk. However, when these fat globules are in their natural large-sized state prior to homogenization, they are not easily absorbed by the gut wall. After homogenization, the milk fat is easily absorbed, and the attached XO gains much greater access to the bloodstream.

Some researchers have asserted that XO, after getting into the bloodstream, directly promotes hardening of the arteries by replacing a substance called plasmalogen that is normally found there. The research supporting this connection between XO and hardening of the arteries is not clear-cut, but whether or not there is a definite cause-and-effect relationship between the two should not be a critical factor in deciding whether you should drink milk. This possible XO link to heart disease is but one more potential connection of milk to disease and premature death. The other factors already cited should be more than enough to convince you to shun milk as a beverage, which is the form of consumption that will do the most damage to the most people.

OTHER DAIRY PRODUCTS

What about yogurt, cheese, sour cream, and any of the many other dairy products? Remember that it is difficult to end up with anything much better or significantly different than that with which you start. When you start with highly processed milk, you cannot magically end up with another dairy product that is substantially more nutritious than its defective precursor.

Having said this, let me add that whole, fat-rich cream has less negatives than the more water-based milk upon which it floats when the milk has not been subjected to homogenization. The cream will contain fewer hormones, antibiotics, pesticides, and other contaminants than the milk below it. The pasteurization still alters the cream, but the effects are less profound. The good news is that you need not avoid either cream or butter. Butter is directly derived from cream, sharing its fatty nature and lessened toxicity relative to other dairy products. The last chapter will address some practical approaches to incorporate a limited amount of dairy into the diet for those who wish to do so. Don't forget, however, that milk and dairy products, except for the naturally fatty butter and cream, combine very poorly with almost all other foods, so be careful not to "double the damage" that you could be doing to yourself by poorly digesting another good food through a bad combination with dairy. If you are going to have the dairy, have it by itself.

FINAL COMMENTS

As toxic as milk is to the many who drink it regularly, milk could be a valuable nutrient if modern technology would leave it and the cow that produced it alone. Sadly, it seems unlikely that this will ever happen. Worldwide food shortages along with an ever-increasing world population are ongoing, significant factors that will continue to argue for more milk production as a cheap source of nutrition. Any measure that would decrease the volume of milk that the dairy industry is now capable of generating would not likely gain much support when so much of the world is starving. Even if pasteurization and homogenization were to eventually end as regular practices, the growth hormone stimulation of dairy cow milk production should continue to receive strong support from most sectors.

Regardless of why things are happening as they are, you still deserve to know the scientific truth about milk, as well as about all the other sources of nutrition that you eat on a daily basis. The truth is still the truth, and you deserve to make choices with as much valid information as you can gather.

CHOLESTEROL: THE GREAT MYTH

CHOLESTEROL AND HEART DISEASE

Much of what we are told by our most trusted authorities ends up being the exact OPPOSITE of what is true and should be heeded. And this isn't to say that the people telling us these "facts" are lying to us. That's a value judgment that cannot fairly be made. But the fact remains that the public often ends up with the worst possible advice that it can be given. This advice is typically far worse than no "guidance" from the authorities at all. Typical examples of this "opposite" advice include the promotion of water fluoridation, the promotion of mercury amalgam fillings, the promotion of commercially available milk as a positive nutrient, and even the promotion of margarine over butter in the diet.

"Avoid foods that are high in cholesterol." This is yet another example of thoroughly misguided advice from our so-called health authorities.

The irrational attack on the effects of cholesterol on health has resulted primarily from the chronic misinterpretation of statistical data. High cholesterol levels are statistically associated with higher rates of heart disease. This is a fact that has been conclusively demonstrated. However, a statistical association does *not* mean there is a cause-and-effect relationship. Cause-and-effect means there is an association, but an association alone does not assure cause-and-effect. Just because the police consistently show up at the scene of a crime doesn't mean that you can later conclude that the police committed the crime. But if we were to use the same statistical reasoning in this police example as modern science uses in the cholesterol–heart disease relationship, we could proceed directly to this ridiculous conclusion without any further thought. If a factor is actually protecting against an unhealthy (and usually unperceived) force, and that factor reliably emerges when that force is present, that factor and not the unhealthy, hidden force will typically get blamed for the damage. This is especially so when the unhealthy force has never really been discovered or recognized. Just like the police at the crime scene, you simply cannot conclude that the paramedics must have initially hurt the victims they are trying to save just because they are physically present with the victims.

Yet this faulty reasoning is precisely what we encounter in the case of cholesterol. The scientific literature has consistently and reliably correlated elevated cholesterol levels with increased coronary heart disease. Further, multiple clinical trials in which cholesterol levels were medically lowered resulted in the reduction of coronary heart disease. These trials have convinced the medical establishment that there must be a cause-and-effect relationship between cholesterol and heart disease. To a very limited degree, there is some truth to this concept. But as we shall see, cholesterol is much more a good guy than a bad guy, protecting the body far more than harming the body.

Even though the cholesterol-lowering trials have demonstrated that lower coronary heart disease death rates correlate with lower cholesterol levels, increases in deaths from a variety of noncardiac causes have also been noted as the cholesterol levels have been lowered. Golomb reviewed many of these trials and found a statistically significant increase in deaths resulting from suicide, accidents, and violence as cholesterol levels were lowered.[1] And these increases in death essentially equaled the decreases in death from coronary heart disease! Therefore, when viewed in terms of ultimate survival, the reduction in cardiac deaths from lowering cholesterol was offset by the increase in deaths from noncardiac causes. No net survival benefit could be claimed from the reduction of cholesterol with medication.

Furthermore, this net lack of survival benefit from cholesterol-lowering drugs does not even take into account any of the side effects of taking such medication. Lazarou et al. published a study that showed that in the United States in 1994, adverse drug reactions were the sixth-leading cause of death.[2] The data did not even include another 2.2 million patients who were seriously injured by their prescription medications. Also not included was the fact that roughly equal numbers of patients died or were seriously injured due to errors of their health care providers. But don't avoid seeing your doctor. Just know that no treatment program comes without cutting both ways. Be an active partner with your health care practitioner in whatever therapies that you take or undergo.

As with nearly all prescription drugs, the commonly prescribed anticholesterol preparations have a large number of potentially significant negative effects on an individual's blood chemistries and overall health. This latest generation of cholesterol-lowering drugs, known collectively as "statins," produces undesirable side effects as often as one-third of the time, depending upon the particular statin chosen. Statins are designed to interfere with the normal function of the liver in its natural synthesis of cholesterol. These drugs so effectively interfere with this normal liver function that the *Physicians' Desk Reference* advises under its warnings for statins that liver function tests be performed routinely before and indefinitely during therapy.

A better general rule of thumb in any approach to the treatment of any disease is to attempt to eliminate the process causing the disease rather than interrupt the body's natural response to that disease process. It's okay to treat disease symptoms, but not to the exclusion of treating the reason why the disease is there in the first place.

High cholesterol levels develop in response to the presence of toxins; the toxins are neutralized by the cholesterol. It follows that the removal of those toxins is the most reasonable way to lower elevated cholesterol levels. Furthermore, the effect of statins on the liver also serves to lower the levels of metabolites other than cholesterol. One of these is coenzyme Q10, a substance vital to the production of energy in all the cells of the body. Not unexpectedly, fatigue can be seen in patients who take these cholesterol-lowering drugs. This can be explained not only by the lower levels of coenzyme Q10, but also by the fact that the lowered cholesterol levels result in less neutralization of circulating toxins.

Since I am a cardiologist, some readers might wonder what my recommendations might be for the individual who has a cholesterol level above 300 milligrams per deciliter (mg%) with a fairly strong family history for cardiac disease. I would probably prescribe a statin or other cholesterol-lowering drug on a short-term basis. In a study by Shih et al., mice exposed to pesticide poisoning who were deliberately fed a high-fat, high-cholesterol diet were more susceptible to developing fatty plaques in their arteries, the type of condition that leads to heart attacks.[3] This suggests that very high cholesterol levels, even though they protect against toxicity, can still directly promote arterial blockages. The body's protective mechanisms can possess their own toxicity when they are exaggerated enough and chronic enough. Therefore, I do not summarily dismiss lowering very high cholesterol levels with medication.

However, I would not choose to lower anyone's levels below 240 to 250 mg%, and I would simultaneously attempt to remove and/or neutralize as much toxicity as possible. This is not to say that I consider a cholesterol level of 240 to 250 mg% optimal. Rather, it is as low as I would choose to go as long as there was significant toxicity present that needed elimination or neutralization. When toxin levels have been minimized, most people will tend to end up with a cholesterol level between 160 and 220 mg%. Such levels generally will not be reached until all significant dental toxins have been removed and the gut is functioning as nontoxically as possible, with good foods properly combined and properly digested. Some high-quality meats must be included in these foods, since a vegetarian diet will not generally sustain cholesterol levels high enough to neutralize one's daily toxin exposure. And although many supplements could be used to boost immune function that will be discussed later, one supplement that would have to be used regularly in high dosage would be vitamin C. It would best be taken as sodium ascorbate powder, in divided doses totaling about 10 to 15 grams daily, as a very general guideline only. For those with kidney disease or those who do not keep themselves well-hydrated with adequate water on a daily basis, the dose should be lower. For those who get diarrhea from oral vitamin C, the dose should be kept below that provoking level, unless the diarrhea is tolerable, since both the toxin-neutralizing effects of the vitamin C in the gut and the more rapid bowel transit times are highly desirable. Of course, these suggestions and any others throughout this book should only be done in cooperation with your chosen health care provider. No blanket suggestions serve all people well.

Another interesting point regarding statin anticholesterol agents deserves mention. It had always been assumed that the only way heart disease is lessened by such drugs results directly from the lowering of the cholesterol levels and nothing else. However, John et al. discovered that fluvastatin, a specific statin drug, increased the bioavailability of nitric oxide in the arteries.[4] Nitric oxide helps the arteries to expand in caliber, a function that could help prevent heart attacks in much the same way as nitroglycerin and other nitrate drugs given to cardiac patients.

Furthermore, Ridker et al. have recently shown that at least one statin drug significantly reduces levels of C-reactive protein.[5] Inflammation throughout the body has been correlated with higher levels of this C-reactive protein. Consistent with this anti-inflammatory effect, Ross et al. have demonstrated that statin drugs can decrease the incidence of nonfatal stroke.[6] Without further studies, however, there is no way to know for certain which biochemical effect of the statin drug is predominating. The lowering of the cholesterol may be a relatively incidental "side effect" accompanying a more important artery-dilating effect or inflammation-lowering effect.

Perhaps a drug that increases nitric oxide levels without lowering cholesterol levels could decrease cardiac deaths without increasing the noncardiac deaths that are seen when cholesterol levels are lowered. Or perhaps any of a number of known anti-inflammatory drugs could also lower cardiac deaths without elevating noncardiac deaths. Presumably neither of these drug approaches would involve the disadvantage of using statin drugs, where lowering cholesterol levels also reduces the neutralization of toxins.

CHOLESTEROL AND TOXINS

The concept that cholesterol can inactivate or neutralize a wide variety of toxins is not new. In 1981, Alouf identified cholesterol as an inactivator of multiple bacterial toxins.[7] Chi et al. and Watson and Kerr showed that elevation of serum cholesterol actually served as a marker for a number of different toxic exposures.[8,9] Studies by Kossman et al. and Bloomer et al. even demonstrated that exposure to the toxicity of pesticides would reliably elevate the cholesterol levels of those exposed individuals.[10,11] Davies et al. also showed that dogs exposed to low levels of methylmercury developed progressively higher levels of cholesterol in the blood over time.[12] A very reasonable conclusion from all of these studies considered together is that cholesterol serves as a defense mechanism to protect the body from a wide range of toxic exposures.

When patients who presented with high cholesterol levels (over 240 mg%) had their mercury amalgams and sources of dental infection removed, these levels usually dropped dramatically within a few days. Generally, the only exceptions occurred in patients who initiated an unforeseen rapid rate of detoxification after the dental revision. A rapid rate of detoxification can keep blood toxin levels elevated. This in turn will usually stimulate the continued elevation of blood cholesterol levels. When such a brisk detoxification is present, cholesterol levels remained elevated for a longer period of time, apparently helping to protect the body from the toxins being released from internal tissue storage sites. Even in the case of these patients, however, cholesterol levels would nearly always decline dramatically at a later date, as the patient continued to detoxify and the detoxification rate and total body toxin load gradually lessened. As long as the toxin levels in the blood declined, the cholesterol levels would also decline.

Remember that both detoxification and new exposure to external toxicity will increase toxin levels in the blood. Cholesterol levels will rise regardless of where the blood toxins originate. And cholesterol levels will drop when these blood toxin levels drop. The cholesterol level, when the diet is not depleted of cholesterol and cholesterol-forming building blocks, as in a vegetarian diet, appears to be an almost ideal laboratory test to track the presence and degree of blood-borne toxins.

A little-appreciated but also well-documented fact is that low serum cholesterol levels are associated with an increased incidence of cancer. This has been demonstrated in many different studies, including those by Schatzkin et al.,[13] Cowan et al.,[14] Davis et al.,[15] Keys et al.,[16] Gerhardsson et al.,[17] Isles et al.,[18] Kagan et al.,[19] Knekt et al.,[20] Kark et al.,[21] Stemmermann et al.,[22] and Williams et al.[23] Yet there are few doctors or patients who are not happier the lower their cholesterol gets. When one considers the concept of the protective effect that cholesterol provides against toxicity, and when one also considers that many toxins are cancer-causing agents, this increased incidence of cancer seen with lower levels of cholesterol makes a lot of sense. The lower your cholesterol goes, the less protection you have against any of the cancer-causing toxins that are circulating in your bloodstream.

It is also of interest to note that Simon and Hudes found that gall-stones are only half as common in women with high blood levels of vitamin C as they are in women with moderate blood levels of vita-min C.[24] Since vitamin C is highly effective in neutralizing the toxi-city from many different sources, it is not surprising that the same unneutralized toxins that can cause cancer can also promote other chronic degenerative diseases, such as gallbladder disease.

The concept of cholesterol protection against toxins gets even fur-ther support from what is known about the chronic effects of low-grade mercury exposure—which is seen in most of the population because they are exposed to mercury from amalgam fillings. Al-though this low-grade chronic mercury exposure (micromercurial-ism) can have a wide variety of effects in different people, irritability, depression, and lessened muscular coordination are among the most common ones. We saw earlier that medically low-ering cholesterol levels increased the number of deaths from vio-lence, suicides, and accidents.

Recently Haley noted that Gulf War veterans had suffered excess postwar deaths both from suicide and from motor vehicle acci-dents.[25] Cumulative toxicity would explain this observation nicely. When enough toxicity finally overwhelms the toxin-neutralizing mechanisms of the body, the baseline toxicity that the Gulf War vet-erans share with most of the rest of the world faces much less op-position. If elevated cholesterol levels are trying to counteract the toxic effects that so many people are experiencing from the contin-ual exposure to the mercury in their amalgam fillings, perhaps low-ering those protective cholesterol levels is allowing irritability to progress into fatal acts of violence, depression into suicide, and decreased muscular coordination into fatal highway accidents. This could also account for the increased incidence of noncardiac deaths in the cholesterol-lowering clinical trials—a finding that has never been scientifically explained. Just because a finding cannot be easily explained does not mean that it can be ignored. A death is a death, whether it comes from a heart attack or a self-inflicted gunshot wound.

Back in 1972, Eastwood and Trevelyan published research that showed that psychological symptoms were associated with an increased risk for physical disorders.[26] There is further support for this hypothesis in the current literature. The Johns Hopkins Precursors Study began in late 1948. Nearly 1,200 medical students were enrolled. Many of them were followed over several decades. Recently, men in the study who reported suffering clinical depression were found to be much more likely to develop coronary artery disease as men who did not suffer depression. Ford et al. concluded that depression is an independent risk factor for coronary heart disease.[27] Another study, by Barefoot and Schroll, conducted over a twenty-seven-year period, also concluded that increased depression was associated with increased risks for heart attack and death from *all* causes.[28] Depression is a very common symptom of unneutralized toxicity, such as is commonly seen with the chronic low-grade exposure from mercury amalgam fillings. When toxicity goes unneutralized, more depression and a greater chance of death from multiple causes is exactly what can be anticipated. And low cholesterol levels allow more toxicity, such as from mercury, to remain unneutralized. It would appear that this may very well be why depression is an independent risk factor for coronary heart disease. Depression is merely an especially common symptom seen in individuals with unneutralized toxicity.

Another study supporting this concept was published by von Ammon Cavanaugh et al.[29] They found that a history of depression was an independent predictor of in-hospital death among the medical inpatients. This further increases the plausibility of the argument that one or more toxins are resulting in both the depression and the fatal disease, since most toxins will nonspecifically cause or aggravate a wide variety of disease processes. Neeleman et al. also recently published research that showed that people at risk for suicide (who are often those individuals who are most depressed) were also at risk for dying prematurely from accidents as well as other illness.[30] We saw earlier that lowered cholesterol levels increase the death rates from suicide as well as accidents. Once again, these statistical correlations can easily be reconciled by focusing on the effects of unneutralized toxicity throughout the body. Suicide doesn't always result from a mind that has inexplicably gone haywire. Much more often, it results from a mind and a nervous system that cannot deal with being poisoned.

THE IMPORTANCE OF CHOLESTEROL IN THE DIET

Now that the little-recognized toxin-fighting role of cholesterol has been clearly demonstrated, let's reexamine the dietary sources of this much-maligned substance. Simply put, plant-based foods lack cholesterol, while meats and other animal-derived foods contain cholesterol. While it is true that the body can make about two-thirds of the cholesterol that it requires, dietary cholesterol is vital to attaining optimal protective cholesterol levels. This means that there must be some animal-based foods in the diet.

Among the severely ill patients who underwent Total Dental Revision, vegetarians rarely showed any substantial clinical improvement. This was probably due to the inability of a body deprived of cholesterol and some of its immediate dietary building blocks to deal with the increased levels of toxins that appeared in the blood from the brisk detoxification typically seen in such patients. In any event, the observation was so reliable that patients who did not want to eat any meat at all were discouraged from even undergoing the dental revision. Whenever a patient invests time, money, and some degree of suffering in a dental and lifestyle treatment plan, they want to get better. And when they don't get better, they get upset and want to blame someone other than themselves. Both doctor and patient want to avoid such a situation from ever occurring. A vegetarian who won't convert may benefit from the removal of highly toxic dental infections, such as root canals, but the rate of detoxification typically seen after a Total Dental Revision will often overwhelm the limited toxin-neutralizing capacity of exclusively vegetarian-based nutrition.

Animal-based foods are also important for optimal nutrition for another reason besides the cholesterol content. The body responds to the presence of toxins by making proteins that will directly bind and help to neutralize those toxins in the bloodstream. When the diet is well balanced, not only cholesterol rises to match an increased toxin presence. Serum globulin levels will typically rise as well. Undoubtedly other protective serum proteins show a similar response, but standard laboratory testing doesn't usually measure serum proteins other than globulin and albumin, the most common blood proteins.

The importance of choice of food relates to what is required to build new blood proteins. New protein must continually be made for the body to prosper, and this protein requires minimal amounts of an adequate variety of amino acid building blocks. Animal-based foods contain amino acids in the proper amounts and ratios to allow the easy synthesis of these protective blood proteins. And the individual amounts, not just the presence, of all the amino acids are very important.

A thoughtful combination of vegetables might provide all the necessary amino acids, but it is enormously difficult for a vegetarian diet to supply adequate amounts of each amino acid to allow optimal synthesis of new proteins. If you are building a house that requires equal amounts of twenty different materials, you simply cannot build the house properly if you have large amounts of eighteen of the materials, but only small amounts of two of the materials. You may still be able to build the house, but it won't be according to plan.

Vegetarians can make protein, but the protein simply cannot have the same three-dimensional configuration when made with chronically depleted levels of any of the vital amino acids. Such proteins are physically different from the proteins built from a diet containing meat protein. Just like keys fitting in locks, they will not have the same ability to bind toxins as proteins of an entirely different physical appearance, or morphology. Proteins often exist as isomers that have the same chemical composition on paper but are physically mirror images of each other. One can have profound biological activity, and the other can be biologically inactive. So, just seeing a normal level of protein on a blood test does not tell you whether the protein is capable of doing an adequate toxin-neutralizing job. Similarly, no blood test should ever be overinterpreted to justify a treatment protocol. A lymphocyte count may be normal, but an additional test might show that a significant percent of the count is nonviable, or dead. When toxins end up adequately eliminated and neutralized, almost all laboratory tests will eventually show improvement along with clinical improvement.

A further shortcoming of vegetables relative to animal-based foods is that they lack adequate amounts of a wide variety of vitamins and minerals. A plant of just about any kind requires only minimal amounts of certain vitamins and minerals to survive to maturity, while animals are much more dependent on a greater nutrient content in the diet to survive to maturity. Nonorganically raised fruits and vegetables can be virtually depleted of essential vitamins and minerals. Pesticides affect both the produce grown and the animals that eat it. When both produce and animals are raised organically, the situation improves, but the vitamin and mineral content of animal-based food is still superior.

Bioavailability of these nutrients is also critical. Many vegetarian diets feature tempeh and miso, two soy-based foods. Although vitamin B_{12} is present in these foods, it is not present in as readily absorbable a form as it is in a number of animal-based foods. It is not enough for some nutrients to just be present in the foods you eat. And it is not enough for a substance felt to be nutritious to just be highly absorbable. Real nutrients must be present in the proper bioavailable form *before* they are absorbed in the gut and then distributed throughout the body. The concept of bioavailability versus mere absorbability is addressed in greater detail in chapter 8. Just looking at the labeled vitamin and mineral content of a food can be misleading when determining whether you are really meeting your body's daily nutrient needs. Meat and vegetables must complement each other, not exclude each other. As you might be suspecting by now, staying healthy is unfortunately not a simple matter in today's world.

Both vegetarians and dedicated meat eaters can be very emotional in the defense of their eating habits. The above recommendations are based exclusively on what has been observed to consistently result in clinical improvement and better blood chemistries. Do remember, however, what was already emphasized in the material presented on food combining. Food must be properly digested to be of benefit. Meat that rots to any degree can be highly toxic. Very few individuals could ever completely and properly digest 12 ounces of meat at a sitting. Our digestive capacities are easily overwhelmed, and most people have some degree of food rotting to go along with proper digestion. The recommendation of meat in the diet assumes small portions of meat, properly combined with compatible vegetables. For most people, no more than 3 to 5 ounces of meat should be eaten at a sitting. For many people, this amount is more than enough for the day. However, greater total daily amounts of meat can be eaten as long as this amount per meal is not exceeded. On the other hand, 3 ounces of meat per meal for some people would still be too much if your gut cannot be encouraged to digest it properly.

Some people won't even require meat daily in order to optimize their health. There should be only a very few people that absolutely require more meat protein than outlined above, and their attention to digestive detail would have to be *scrupulous* to prevent the excess meat from rotting in the gut. The optimal plan of nutrition must ultimately be empirical. You start with what helps most people, but you never ignore individualized needs and sensitivities.

The only vegetarians who should remain vegetarians are those who choose not to eat meat for religious reasons—or simply because they love animals. For such individuals, organic produce is a must, and they should also be keenly aware of what amino acids are present in which vegetables and in what amounts. The perfect vegetarian diet seems to sustain the individual who has been spared the large toxic challenge routinely faced by most people. However, as I have already suggested, overcoming established illness in the face of daily toxicity is nearly impossible for even the best-designed of vegetarian regimens.

BUTTER VERSUS MARGARINE

From a health standpoint, there is an enormous difference between butter and margarine. The only reason to choose margarine would be that you actually prefer its taste to that of butter, and your budget is limited. If you don't want to eat butter, for whatever reason, don't make it worse by eating margarine. With margarine, you are just adding one more toxic factor into your internal bodily environment—a factor that could easily be avoided.

Even though butter should never be avoided due to its cholesterol content, its effect on cholesterol levels cannot be understood
independent of one's toxin levels. When patients underwent the removal of dental toxicity, their elevated cholesterol levels would routinely drop in spite of the fact that they were being encouraged to
eat as much butter and as many eggs on a daily basis as they desired. Cholesterol-laden foods raise the blood cholesterol levels only
when toxins are present that need neutralization or inactivation.

In his impressive book, *Nutrition and Physical Degeneration*, Weston Price, D.D.S., repeatedly made the same correlations between
choice of foods and maintenance (or recovery) of health.[31] The in-
clusion of the modern processed foods of the "civilized" populations of the world, refined sugar and white flour, consistently
destroyed the dental and general health of a wide variety of isolated
populations that Dr. Price studied in the early 1930s. Dr. Price personally observed the eating habits and health of fourteen isolated
groups of people in Switzerland, Africa, South America, Australia,
New Zealand, Polynesia, and North America. He found that simple,
unrefined foods sustained health. Raw butter and other raw dairy
foods produced from properly raised cows and goats would often
single-handedly reverse advanced diseases in the individuals who
were able to quit eating sugar and white flour. It should be noted
that Dr. Price never observed total vegetarianism among any of the
healthy groups, although they all ate meat far less frequently than
most Americans do today.

Margarine, a creation of the scientific laboratory, really bears no
resemblance to butter, except in appearance. And this appearance
is due to the yellow dye that is added to the white margarine to
convince consumers that they really are consuming a legitimate
"substitute" for butter. Incredibly, in the 1930s, margarine was
actually sold with a packet of yellow dye that the consumer could
mix in with the margarine to complete the butter masquerade.
Today's margarines are commonly based on a number of cheap oils,

including soybean, corn, canola, and cottonseed oils. These oils typically have had all of the nutrient value extracted or processed out of them. Nearly all of the proteins, fiber, minerals, lecithin, and other desirable natural components have been removed. Most of the vitamins are also gone.

To make matters worse, the oil that is used to make margarine is first typically hydrogenated to turn it from a liquid into a solid, forming many toxic substances in the process. Margarines then end up with a large amount of what is known as *trans*-fatty acids in them. These *trans*-fatty acids have been associated with increased disease and compromise of the cardiovascular system, immune system, and reproductive system. I never cease to be amazed that there is still probably not one coronary care unit in any hospital in the United States that even offers its patients the option of butter over this harmful synthetic spread.

Butter, when it comes from a quality source, maintains a high food value. Even when coming from pasteurized cream, butter still maintains a positive food value, in sharp contrast to pasteurized milk and other pasteurized milk products. Perhaps an additional benefit of butter that is less recognized is that its increased use in cooking also keeps us consuming less of the toxically produced and commonly consumed seed and vegetable oils.

While this may be a bit of an oversimplification, I maintain that limiting yourself to olive oil and butter in your cooking is the healthy way to go. Few other readily available oils are without some degree of toxicity. Remember that margarine is at least one source of toxicity that you can easily eliminate from your daily diet.

OILS, FATS, AND NUTS

Seeds, nuts, and vegetables are the sources for most of the nutrient oils that are available today. Like all other foods, oils lose more of their nutritive value the more they are processed. Organic, cold-pressed oils are the only way to go. If you are highly motivated, have a chef's imagination, and want to experiment with different flavors, preparing meals with a wide variety of oils can be a lot of fun, and can take some of the boredom out of your diet. However, if you are not nearly so motivated, don't feel that you will be automatically depleting yourself of nutrition that cannot be obtained elsewhere.

Unless they are organically grown and properly extracted, many oils contain toxins. Not only are the source crops grown with the liberal use of highly toxic pesticides and only slightly less toxic inorganic fertilizers, but the extraction processes typically employ high heat and a variety of toxic chemicals to produce the oils. The final products also have little remaining nutritive value due to the nature of the extraction process. Do not delude yourself into thinking that you are expanding your base of positive nutrition by including a wide variety of nonorganically produced oils in your foods or in their preparation.

While a number of different oils, produced correctly, can be positive additions to your diet, it is very important to realize that nearly all unrefined oils have a low smoke point. For this reason, they are not suitable for high-temperature frying, as the smoke is indicative of destruction of the fatty acids and glycerol that are present. Of course, you should avoid high-temperature frying anyway, because this type of food preparation readily destroys much of the nutrient content, while producing products capable of causing cancer, including free radicals. However, whenever you do prepare food in such a manner, you shouldn't make the entire process even more nutritively negative with the wrong choice of cooking agent.

Butter and olive oil are probably the two best choices for routine cooking and light frying, or sautéing. A somewhat expensive derivative of butter—ghee, or clarified butter—is an even better choice than butter, since it won't burn as easily. If organically produced, almond, hazelnut, and sesame oils can also be used for baking and sautéing. Other organic vegetable and nut oils, such as canola, flax, pistachio, pumpkin, safflower, sunflower, and walnut, should generally just be consumed in salads or added to food after it is cooked. While safflower and sunflower oils can also be used in baking, it is probably easiest to get used to a few comfortable oil choices for cooking and to approach the remainder of good oils as another form of supplementation.

Just as with fruits and fruit juices, it is always best to eat whole food and properly digest it to get optimal nutrition. Eating fresh nuts, seeds, and vegetables will also be more desirable than just adding their extracted oils to other foods or just taking those oils directly as nutritional supplements. Nuts and seeds are excellent single-item snacks, and you should go for the raw ones rather than the roasted ones whenever possible.

CLOSING NOTES

I feel it is important as this chapter is concluded to make an additional comment to all who choose to follow a vegetarian lifestyle. I truly admire anyone who either has a strong enough religious conviction against the consumption of animal flesh or simply a strong enough love and respect for the animal kingdom that they don't eat these foods. But I must also add that everything I advocate stems from direct and repeated clinical observations, as well as many scientific studies, of which I have cited but a few. When one food makes blood chemistries improve and another food has no effect or even worsens blood chemistries, I will empirically support the food that improves blood chemistries. I am only reporting what appear to be scientifically well-founded concepts. If your religion prevents you from eating meat, then so be it. But if your vegetarianism is based on the idea that avoiding animal-based foods is the healthiest possible diet to eat, I would respectfully suggest that such a notion is completely wrong and will be detrimental to your health in the long run, if not sooner.

SEAFOOD: ANOTHER SOURCE OF TOXINS

METHYLMERCURY

Seafood doesn't have to be a source of toxicity, but the unfortunate fact is that it usually does contain significant toxins. Methylmercury, an organic form of mercury that is vastly more toxic clinically than inorganic mercury or elemental mercury, is selectively concentrated in most fish and shellfish. This is why methylmercury is the contaminant of primary concern in seafood. However, throughout the nation seafood from both fresh and salt waters is significantly contaminated not only with methylmercury, but also with other highly toxic substances, including polychlorinated biphenyls (PCBs), dioxins, and chlorinated pesticides. In fact, if your seafood comes from a heavily industrialized area, methylmercury can actually be the minor contaminant.

The toxicity of ingested methylmercury has been very well documented. The original epidemiological treatment of methylmercury poisoning occurred in Minamata, Japan, between 1953 and 1960, after a chemical company had been dumping tons of mercury into Minamata Bay for about three decades. Six hundred and twenty-eight people were studied, with seventy-eight deaths attributed directly to the poisoning. In addition, thousands of people living around the bay sustained some degree of poisoning from eating the highly contaminated fish. The most common clinical manifestations of the poisoning were tingling sensations, tremors, muscle weakness, slurred speech, tunnel vision, hearing loss, unsteady walking, and other sensory disturbances. Autopsy studies revealed striking brain degeneration, with losses of almost 50 percent of the normal volume and weight of the brain tissue noted. Perhaps the most disturbing of the effects of this toxicity occurred in the womb. In all instances reviewed, congenital exposure resulted in a substantially higher incidence of symptoms than resulted when a comparable level of exposure occurred in an adult. In addition to the disturbances already listed, such exposure during fetal development would often substantially delay or even block multiple developmental milestones after birth.

Methylmercury poisoning returned to the spotlight in 1971, when an unknown but large number of Iraqi people ate tainted bread. Methylmercury-treated seed grain had been used in the making of this homemade bread. Bakir et al. were but one of the groups who published their study of this population.[1] All of the symptoms noted in Minamata were again seen in the adults consuming large amounts of this bread. However, those exposed in the womb again showed the greatest sensitivity. Some congenitally exposed infants were afflicted with cerebral palsy, altered muscle tone, and delayed onset of the ability to walk.

It is important to emphasize at this point that a couple of the best ways to deal with an acute methylmercury exposure are vitamin C, N-acetylcysteine (NAC), and bioavailable forms of selenium. Vitamin C can be given both orally to bowel tolerance (onset of loose diarrhea or abdominal cramping) and intravenously in a dose of 50 to 60 grams over several hours. This dose can be repeated as needed, and it can reach a cumulative dose of up to 200 grams daily for a few days if the toxic exposure is severe enough. NAC can also be given along with the vitamin C.

Ballatori et al. have published data showing that mice drinking water with NAC will excrete roughly 50 percent of an administered load of methylmercury over a forty-eight-hour period, while the control animals without NAC would only excrete only 5 to 10 percent of that load.[2] NAC can be taken regularly in doses of 600 to 1,200 milligrams daily, and several grams a day for a few days can be taken when the methylmercury exposure is known to be high. NAC is also believed to exert a protective effect against methylmercury for the growing fetus. Ornaghi et al. found that the effect of NAC was highly effective in blocking the ability of methylmercury in mice to either reduce fetus weight or cause fetal death.[3]

Selenium is known to bind to methylmercury. However, unlike NAC, it does not promote mercury excretion. In fact, selenium supplements do not lower the mercury levels in animals given methylmercury, and when appropriate amounts of selenium are given, even higher levels of mercury can accumulate without obvious signs of clinical toxicity. It appears, then, that selenium is a neutralizer of mercury toxicity, but it does not promote mercury's elimination from the body. However, do not jump to the conclusion that more selenium is always better. As discussed in greater detail in chapter 8, nearly all supplements can have their own toxicity. Too much needs to be avoided as diligently as too little.

The role that selenium plays in the neutralization of methylmercury might help to explain the variable clinical toxicity of fish and other seafood. Hagmar et al. showed that fishermen who had the highest fish intake also had the highest blood levels of selenium.[4] It seems likely that the methylmercury content in some seafood will be less well "matched" with selenium in its edible flesh than other seafood. Although the amount of unneutralized mercury may not yet have poisoned the fish that ingested it, this fraction can be expected to be much more toxic to the human who eats the fish, since fish appear to be far less sensitive to consumed mercury than are humans. Conversely, some fish that are consumed might deliver its mercury in a more neutralized condition, with little apparent clinical toxicity in the consuming human. Furthermore, the actual content of mercury in fish and other forms of seafood can be highly variable, and larger ingested amounts of mercury, whether bound to selenium or not, can be expected to be more harmful and toxic in the long run.

The sensitivity of the person eating the seafood must also be considered. When your immune system has been sensitized to "protect" you from additional ingested mercury, secondary immune reactions can make you very ill when you eat seafood that contains even a small amount of this toxin. And when the immune system is just very weak from long-term toxic abuse and poor nutrition and unable to deal even with minor amounts of new toxins, fish and seafood can prove to be highly toxic meals. It must also be remembered that since selenium does not promote mercury excretion, body levels of mercury will continue to accumulate over time. Even if selenium is bound to the stored mercury, a point will be reached when that storage capacity will eventually be overwhelmed. At that point, toxic symptoms will appear.

Perhaps one of the most significant considerations is that greater amounts of stored mercury will result in greater amounts of released mercury when detoxification mechanisms are later stimulated. Many people do not even concern themselves with toxins and detoxification until they get a little older and begin to realize that they won't live forever. For this reason, the reemergence of the stored mercury as the body detoxifies will be even more toxic clinically in these people, because their immune systems will typically have been stressed and traumatized for a longer time, and immune protection against toxins will be lessened.

It is especially important for pregnant women to entirely eliminate their fish and seafood consumption. Although untainted seafood may have substantial nutritive value, it is difficult to have enough nutritive value to counterbalance the effects of any needless fetal exposure to additional methylmercury. Drexler and Schaller found that mercury levels in breast milk were directly and positively associated with fish consumption.[5] Furthermore, they found that the mother's consumption of fish appeared to be a larger contributor of mercury to the breast milk than the presence of her mercury amalgam fillings.

PCBs

PCBs demonstrate a clinical toxicity that is very similar to that seen with methylmercury. Neurological problems and reproductive problems are prominent toxic effects. Children born of sufficiently exposed mothers had increased prematurity, growth retardation, decreased intelligence, and less efficient nerve function. Great Lakes fish have long been contaminated with PCBs. In the 1960s, it was first noted that these noxious chemicals accumulate in the fish. It was then noted that the fish-eating birds in the Great Lakes area also exhibited reproductive problems. Further analysis led to the discovery that literally hundreds of different chemical contaminants maintained a presence in the fish. It wasn't really formally recognized until the late 1980s that humans were accumulating these contaminants as well. In retrospect, this should not have been so amazing. After all, you literally are what you eat. If you are at the top of the food chain, you are the repository of all of the bioaccumulation that takes place below you.

WHAT TO DO

The primary problem with just eliminating seafood completely from your diet is that in so doing you eliminate a major source of inexpensive, tasty, and otherwise nutritious protein. Also, in spite of the increasing availability of organic meats and produce, it would seem that all of our other sources of animal protein are becoming *increasingly* contaminated as each year goes by, thanks to the unrelenting use of pesticides, antibiotics, hormones, and other chemicals and drugs in raising livestock. Another source of toxicity is the fish meal that is variably used in the feeding of chickens, cows, pigs, and fish. Fish meal tends to be a bit pricey relative to other feeds, so the percent of fish meal in the diets of these animals tends to remain on the low side. Pigs and chickens get fed fish meal more frequently than the cows. However, what any animal is fed is highly variable from one farmer to the next, depending on financial considerations and a given farmer's philosophy on the raising of farm animals. Just remember that no plant or animal will magically destroy the pesticide or heavy metal that was contained in its food. It simply gets kicked up one notch higher on the food chain.

Only the purest of organic fertilization should be used in the raising of crops. This would provide food animals with a much higher quality of nutrition, and it would prevent many toxins from entering the food chain. Once they are present, toxins—unlike the vitamin and mineral content of harvested foods—are not easily depleted or neutralized, and they are rarely eliminated from the food chain. The only way to avoid having significant toxicity in our foods, including seafood, is to make sure that toxins never get the opportunity to enter the food chain in the first place. As a practical point, however, this goal will never be reached in the case of seafood until we can exercise complete control over the growth environment of the fish from hatching to harvesting. Nothing will make seafood harvested from the oceans or our many lakes and rivers completely safe to eat.

At this point, you are probably thinking that you just can't win, and that you are going to encounter toxicity regardless of what you eat. To a limited degree, that is true. However, the purpose of this chapter, and this entire book, is to *minimize* toxicity as much as possible. There is no nontoxic way to eat, and there is no nontoxic way to live. But your immune system is capable of dealing with a lot, and if you keep working to minimize the stresses that are placed on your immune system, you will be rewarded with better health for a longer time.

When it comes to seafood, then, what should you do? Practically speaking, there is no magic amount of seafood that is definitely safe to eat. Since methylmercury and other toxins found in seafood can gradually accumulate in your body over time, the fact that you don't get ill when you eat the seafood doesn't mean that the toxins you consume won't make you ill later. Probably the best advice regarding seafood (if you are a reasonably healthy, seafood-loving person) is to have it no more than two to three times a month, eating no more than 4 to 5 ounces at a sitting. However, this recommendation is just a compromise that pertains only if you must have some seafood in your diet, and you have determined that you will not give it up.

Speaking globally, much of the world would starve if seafood was eliminated as a food source. As a relatively inexpensive source of protein and other positive nutrients, seafood will remain a substantial percentage of the diet of very many people. However, such a situation does not change the unfortunate facts about the overall toxicity of seafood. The motivated reader of this book has the right to know, as completely as possible, about the healthiest way to eat and about the dietary toxins that can be minimized or avoided. So, if you aren't hopelessly in love with the taste of seafood, the best advice is to avoid eating it completely.

THE NEED FOR WATER

OVERVIEW

Everyone knows they need water to stay healthy, or, for that matter, to just survive. What most people do not realize is how much water should be included in their daily regimens. About 70 percent of our bodies is composed of water, and it is absolutely essential that we drink enough water to keep our bodies healthy. Most people hardly drink much more than 20 to 30 percent of the amount of water that they really should be drinking every day.

Coffee and soda are not substitutes for water, even though they have a high water content. In fact, they are detrimental to our health in many ways, in addition to satisfying the thirst that should be satisfied with pure water. Even fruit and vegetable juices are not substitutes for water.

As we shall see, water is involved in many important functions in the body, and repeatedly quenching your daily thirst with beverages other than water will eventually take its toll. By doing this, you can actually cause your body to become dehydrated, even though you may be consuming substantial amounts of liquid. This is because some drinks, such as coffee and alcohol, act as diuretics which cause a net loss of water from the body.

THIRST

A seemingly rational approach to water is to drink when you are thirsty. However, significant thirst occurs after your body has already become dehydrated to some degree. The goal of proper hydration is achieved when you can get into the habit of chronically drinking water regularly enough and in large enough amounts that you never become distracted with overwhelming thirst.

If you ignore thirst often enough in your daily lifestyle, you will eventually lose the ability to be properly sensitive to varying levels of dehydration throughout your body. You may survive, but you will make just about every cellular task that your body must perform more difficult. Eventually, these cellular tasks will not be performed completely, resulting in the appearance of new diseases or the worsening of old diseases. Either through this ignoring of thirst or through the natural aging process, or both, the thirst mechanism is consistently seen to lessen and even fail as we become older. In fact, increasing age is directly associated with a steadily decreasing water content in the cells of the body. Such a steady decline in the cellular water content may well be a significant independent reason for the acceleration of the aging process.

Interestingly, the desire for salt in the food, which can indirectly affect one's state of hydration, may be induced prenatally by maternal dehydration. Crystal and Bernstein found that infants whose mothers experienced moderate to severe morning sickness along with moderate to severe vomiting during pregnancy craved salt more than infants whose mothers had not experienced morning sickness.[1] Although the explanation for this phenomenon was not clear, it was hypothesized that the fluctuations in fluid and electrolyte balance resulting from the dehydration could be related to the activation of hormones that triggered the salt cravings. In any case, this study reinforces the concept that the mechanisms of thirst and dehydration are not as straightforward as we may think. Furthermore, it appears that chronically stressing the body by drinking too little water can have far-reaching physiological effects.

BASIC FUNCTIONS

Although it might just seem like common sense to appreciate that you can't shortchange the body requirements for adequate daily amounts of pure water, it is useful to outline just what water does for you. The many enzymes in your body, which are essential for regulating just about every life function, work more effectively when the cellular fluid is not too thick. It becomes too thick when your body lacks adequate water. Water is literally the solvent in which every one of your body's activities takes place. Water is the primary component of all bodily fluids, including blood, lymph, saliva, cerebrospinal fluid, and the body's many glandular secretions. Intestinal, gastric, and pancreatic juices are nearly 98 percent water. The blood supply is about 92 percent water. A person who weighs 150 pounds should contain about 80 quarts of water.

It has even been suggested that some otherwise unexplained pains in the body are caused by "local thirst." This means that there is not enough water present to allow local metabolic functions to take place normally. This then results in an accumulation of incomplete metabolism by-products in a tissue, sometimes resulting in pain or discomfort at that location.

When you consider that urine generally has a fairly limited range of concentration in which toxins can be eliminated, it should come as no surprise that skimping on your water will result in larger amounts of toxins and metabolic by-products that must be excreted. No matter how much water you drink, you will excrete some toxins and waste products every time you urinate. The only compensation that your kidneys can make is to allow an increasingly dilute urine to be formed as your water intake increases. But when you are drinking less rather than more water, the "steady state" of toxins and waste products can lean much more easily toward a net accumulation rather than a net elimination. Once you have formed the habit of drinking too little water, you have laid a foundation that allows wastes and toxins to build up gradually for the rest of your life.

Just as toxins from any source will cause some problems and aggravate all other existing problems, inadequate water intake can be expected to have the same effects. As mentioned above, water is not only essential for proper cellular function throughout your body, it is also essential for the proper excretion of cellular waste products and any other toxins that have found their way into your body. Therefore, poor water intake can be expected to increase your overall bodily toxicity. Good foods, exercise, supplements, meditation, or just about anything else you can think of to support your health will NOT compensate for ignoring this basic bodily requirement. Don't reinvent the wheel; do whatever else you think is good for you, but do not neglect drinking your water.

WHEN TO DRINK

At the start of this book, the concepts of normal digestion and proper food combining were addressed. It was also mentioned that large amounts of water with a meal were not desirable, and could inhibit normal digestion. This is a bit ironic, since many individuals actually think that drinking a lot of water with meals is a good digestive habit. This is not the case. Even though most foods have very large amounts of water in them, the concept of having just enough water in the stomach at the time of digestion must be addressed. As with just about every other rule in human physiology, too much is just as undesirable as too little. Water will certainly be absorbed fairly quickly, but it is still very capable of minimizing or cutting short essential digestive enzyme activity by simple dilution. The less concentrated the enzymes are in the digestive juice surrounding the food, the less rapidly and effectively digestion will proceed. Furthermore, the digestive cells of the stomach lining do not have an unlimited capacity to keep on producing enough additional enzymes to maintain the needed concentrations in the stomach in the face of additional ingested water.

Water is also often consumed with ice, and very cold water will further slow enzyme activity. Within certain ranges, heat reliably accelerates enzyme activity, and cold will reliably slow enzyme activity. Water also dilutes the acid levels in the stomach, further slowing the activity level of the acid-triggered protein-busting enzymes. Thus, *concentration, production,* and *activity* of gastric enzymes are all unfavorably affected by water drinking with meals.

With drinking water, as with so many other things, timing is everything, or at least, timing is very important. Generally, water can be consumed in almost unlimited quantities before a meal, as long as a previous meal or large snack was not eaten too recently. The best time to drink a large amount of water is first thing in the morning, upon arising. Try to drink at least a couple of tall glasses. It doesn't have to be done all at once; you can drink it over whatever period of time elapses until you first eat. If you can, shoot for a quart of water to start off the day. If you have a medical problem that you think might somehow be aggravated by such water consumption, check with your doctor first. However, as discussed above, drinking large amounts of water (between meals) should help most medical problems.

After most meals of moderate size and only minimal to moderate meat protein consumption, you can resume drinking water two to three hours after eating. However, if you indulge in a large amount of steak, you might have to wait four to six hours to resume significant water consumption. All degrees of compromise can be reached in your individual situation. It's okay to take frequent small sips of

water with and immediately following a meal, or you can completely abstain until you drink a full glass of water a few hours later.
You will rapidly learn what amounts of water and what timing of
its drinking relative to your meals will agree with your digestion
best. Whenever you cause a stomach that feels perfectly settled after
a well-combined and properly eaten meal to get even a little bit
upset after drinking your water, then you know your water amount
and timing of drinking are not in sync with your digestion. Typically, too much water will cause a well-settled stomach to develop
gas and belching, along with an acid burning sensation with the
belching. You also may just feel more bloated without any of these
other symptoms.

You should maintain this pattern of water drinking throughout
the day. You certainly should not just drink a huge amount of water
first thing in the morning and quit for the day. How sensitive your
bladder is will determine how close you can continue drinking your
water before going to bed. Remember that you need very little time
before a meal to drink as much water as you want.

DECIDING WHAT TO DRINK

Your water should be as pure as possible. Tap water varies widely
from one city to the next, and well water is even more variable from
one well to the next. The bottom line is that you want as little of any
dissolved substances in your water as possible. For the many reasons outlined in chapter 8 on supplementation, you do NOT want
to drink a lot of mineral-rich waters. One authority estimates that
4,000 to 5,000 gallons of nondistilled water, representing a typical
lifetime's consumption, includes from 200 to 300 pounds of inorganic, dissolved rock-form minerals. These water minerals are not
present in a bioavailable form, even though the body can absorb
them. There may be short-term benefits to be gained from drinking
such water, but it also has long-term accumulative toxic effects.

Enough dissolved rock, as with enough dissolved anything, eventually falls out of solution and deposits. In the case of mineral-rich water, the inorganic minerals can deposit and accumulate throughout the body. Also, since low levels of toxic minerals are often also present in such water, levels of these toxins will also accumulate over the years. Good food and high-quality supplementation should be your primary sources for your minerals.

Chemically softened waters should also be avoided. In addition to the other nonbioavailable minerals that you should be avoiding, these softened waters have huge amounts of sodium or even potassium, far beyond what your body requires. Anyone with enough kidney disease can actually put themselves at risk of life-threatening accumulations of potassium if they use the potassium-based softeners in their water. As it turns out, the chemical softening of water is also completely unnecessary. Proper use of magnets can easily soften water satisfactorily, without the addition of any chemicals. The application of a strong south pole magnetic field to a water pipe softens water naturally. See Appendix II at the end of the book for more information on such magnetic products.

Another commonly heard refrain concerning water is that hard water is better for you than soft water. Statistical studies seem to consistently show that communities consuming hard water have a lower coronary heart disease death rate, as well as a lower rate of strokes. This may be true, but this does NOT address that neither hard nor soft water is being compared to much purer water, such as distilled water or reverse osmosis purified water.

Before rain gets contaminated, it represents nature's way of water distillation and purification. Water is a substance that naturally leaches out the impurities of its surrounding environment. Most substances, toxic or otherwise, will dissolve in water to some degree, given enough time. Just because a water source is "natural" doesn't mean that every attempt shouldn't be made to further purify it as completely as possible.

Hard water does have minerals in it, but these are present in non-food, nonbioavailable forms. If someone is severely mineral-depleted, even these nonbioavailable forms may help for a while. However, hard water is never a good way to treat mineral depletion. Inorganic minerals, such as those found in hard water and rocks, should be excluded from ingestion as completely as possible, and bioavailable mineral sources, such as those found in foods and good supplements, should be used to correct any mineral depletions. Remember what happens to pipes that have carried hard water for many years. They fill up with rocklike mineral deposits, which can sometimes block them off completely. The same thing can happen to your arteries, given enough time and enough non-bioavailable minerals. Keep your arteries and your organs clear, and drink only the purest of water.

Tap water also has two additional enemies: chlorine and fluoride. These highly reactive chemicals create a lot of toxicity in the chronic consumer. It's just one more example of not having a sizeable control group for comparison. The majority of the population that drinks tap water every day continues to dwarf the minority that doesn't. When most people are in the same boat, it's very hard to ever fully evaluate the benefits of avoiding toxic water additives such as chlorine and fluoride.

A few words about fluoride. While all of the information on the toxicity of fluoride could fill many volumes of books, some of the more notorious facts about fluoride toxicity will be highlighted here. For a more extensive treatment of this subject, see *Fluoride: The Aging Factor* by John Yiamouyiannis,[2] from which the following information is taken.

Fluoride, at levels *less* than those currently promoted for the fluoridation of public water supplies, will reliably inhibit DNA repair enzyme activity. Also, fluoride will inhibit the normal use of oxygen by the body, promote free radical formation, and interfere with the immune functions of white blood cells. Fluoride has also been shown to increase the frequency of mutation in the sperm cells of fruit flies exposed to X rays. All of these effects (decreased immune function, decreased cellular use of oxygen, decreased DNA repair enzyme function, and increased level of mutation) can increase the risk of developing cancer. And, in fact, Yiamouyiannis and Burk published a study detailing evidence that points to fluoride as a cancer-causing agent.[3]

Amazingly, fluoride had been mainly used as insect and rat poison before being introduced to the American public water supply. Even if fluoride did prevent tooth decay, which is also highly debatable, there is no justification for the massive administration of such a toxic substance to so many people without their consent. For some reason, public water fluoridation is another political flashpoint for many people and politicians, with name-calling and finger-pointing always overwhelming any rational discussion or scientific review of the case against fluoride. But you have now been warned. Research the issues for yourself before you decide that fluoridated water just has to be beneficial.

Consider avoiding tap water where the fluoride levels are "naturally" high. Know that the fluoride content of fluoridated toothpaste and fluoride treatments administered by your dentist are enormously high relative to fluoridated water, and they should be carefully avoided if you decide that fluoride is not best for you and your family.

Chlorine is another toxin that has gained widespread acceptance. The proponents of chlorine point to its effectiveness at eliminating so many of the microbes in water, claiming that this has greatly reduced the incidence of transmissible infectious diseases. While that may be true, it ignores the fact that water can be purified even more completely of microorganisms with proper ozonation or exposure to ultraviolet light, neither of which entails any known residual toxicity. In his book *Coronaries/Cholesterol/Chlorine*, Joseph M. Price, M.D., makes a compelling case that the chlorine in our water supply contributes significantly to the ever-increasing rate of heart disease.[4] If other better methods of purification are available, why even take the risk of adding anything to your drinking water that can have negative effects on your health?

In general, well water, without purification, should not be your drinking water. Well water is very much a "mixed bag," with little predictability as to which types or what amounts of different contaminants commonly found in our aquifers today will find their way into the well-water sources. Even if you pay a laboratory to have your well water tested, most testing does not cover many of the potential toxins that you can encounter, unless you are willing to spend literally thousands of dollars on such testing. Furthermore, a fairly distant farm could use pesticides at one time of the year and not at another, only getting into your aquifer intermittently. Don't pay a lot of money to give yourself a false sense of security just because you tested your well water at the wrong time of the year.

Well water can also have a highly variable content of minerals, mostly in the nonbioavailable form discussed earlier. Well water may also be contaminated with toxic minerals and heavy metals, especially near mountains and mining areas. However, such contamination is not limited to such areas. Drinking any unpurified well water over a prolonged period of time is just another slow version of Russian roulette. Don't do it.

THE BEST DRINKING WATER

In a nutshell, the purest water that you can get is what you should drink on a regular basis. Probably the purest waters available today are those purified by distillation or reverse osmosis. However, distillation remains the single best way to purify water as completely as possible. Some waters that have been distilled multiple times are also available. These are the best waters for drinking. If they have also been given an ozone or ultraviolet treatment, all the better. Any water, however well purified, can later become contaminated with microorganisms before being consumed.

Note that all bottled waters are not the same. Fortunately, the ones that are distilled or purified by reverse osmosis also tend to be the least expensive. I do not recommend bottled "mountain spring waters." These may have a good taste, but they still risk having some of the mineral and heavy metal contaminants mentioned earlier. There are few, if any, places left on the planet where the water is still so pure that it can just be bottled and sold without concern to the consumer.

Home distillers and reverse osmosis purification units can be purchased if you prefer this convenience to regularly hauling bottled water from the supermarket. Whether this makes sense for you depends upon your budget, and on the amount of water that you drink. If you opt for reverse osmosis water purification, be certain to assure yourself that the toxins and contaminants of concern to you are adequately removed by the model you are considering for purchase.

CONCLUSION

The regular and adequate drinking of pure water is not only an extremely important factor in maintaining good health, it is also one of the easiest factors to incorporate into your lifestyle. Many toxins are difficult and expensive to avoid. Don't pass up the opportunity to eliminate one significant source of toxicity that can be completely and easily avoided without major sacrifice. Drink lots of pure water, and you not only avoid a major source of potential toxicity, you promote good health and the elimination of other toxins.

THE IMPORTANCE OF PROPER SUPPLEMENTATION

OVERVIEW

Nearly all commercially available foods today are depleted of much of their vitamin and mineral content. Often this depletion can be dramatic, with some important nutrients being *completely* absent in the final food or food product. There are a number of reasons for this unfortunate depletion, and the food industry still remains seemingly unconcerned about any of these nutrient-depleting factors.

Most soils have been massively depleted of a number of nutrients. Plants cannot be expected to contain a wide variety of essential minerals when the soil in which they were grown didn't contain them in the first place. Modern chemical fertilizers are very effective in stimulating the growth of basic crops, but the crops that result are nutrient poor. For example, NPK, or nitrogen-phosphorus-potassium fertilizer, can stimulate plant growth even in the absence of other nutrients. This allows successive crops to progressively deplete the soil, even though the crops still appear to prosper. However, even though the resulting vegetable may look robust, it lacks a full range of minerals, vitamins, and other nutrients. It's very difficult to ever end up with more than what you start with! Yet nutrition science seems to ignore these vital issues.

When you add to this initial depletion the depletions that occur in modern food processing, the nutritional value of many of our food staples plummets even further. Canning, freezing, and other methods of storage take a substantial toll on nutrient content. Moreover, nutrients are sometimes removed deliberately. Most grains have had the nutrients stripped out to make refined flours into commercially acceptable breads and cereals. The nutrients are then later sold separately as foods such as wheat germ or utilized as supplements in themselves. When a label says that a food is "enriched," BEWARE. This enrichment is analogous to getting robbed of $100 and being given back $10 by a sympathetic robber. When you receive the $10, you have not been "enriched"; you have only been a bit less massively depleted. Also, as we shall see, the chemical forms of the nutrients that are put back into these depleted foods are often not even beneficial; in fact, they can actually be toxic.

The unfortunate bottom line is that in today's world it is almost impossible to have a diet that will meet all of your nutritional needs. However, recognizing this issue overcomes only the first hurdle in reaching optimal nutrition. Supplements are literally assaulting us daily with ever-rosier promises of how you can get everything that you need. How can you tell which claims are true and what supplements are really best? This chapter will be directed at helping you make this evaluation intelligently, and, hopefully, it will further assist you in your quest for the best of health through optimal nutrition.

BASIC CONCEPTS

Let's start with a few basic definitions. A *supplement* is any preparation designed to help the body reach its optimal state of nutrition. It supplies the vitamins, minerals, and other elements essential to optimal bodily and immune function. Very literally speaking, a supplement is simply supposed to furnish what is lacking. *Minerals*, the focus of many supplements, are nonorganic substances that usually come from the earth's crust. Minerals contain many of the elements essential for cellular function, such as sodium, potassium, magnesium, and calcium. *Vitamins,* also emphasized in many supplements, are largely unrelated organic substances that the body requires in tiny amounts to maintain normal metabolic functioning. Finally, there is a huge variety of other supplements that are unrelated chemically, and are touted to have different effects on the body, based on either scientific evidence or empirical observations. A sampling of such supplements could include coenzyme A, aloe vera, dehydroepiandrosterone (DHEA), pycnogenol, colostrum, saw palmetto, N-acetylcysteine, and methyl-sulfonyl-methane (MSM). Literally, thousands of different such supplements are presently available. The only common thread in this category is that a beneficial effect on the body is felt to occur from the ingestion of these nonvitamin, nonmineral supplements, although they may have their own vitamin and mineral content. They can have hormonal effects, vitamin-like effects, enzyme-helping effects, toxin-neutralizing effects, or immune system–supporting effects. Generally, if you don't take any of these different supplements, you will never be considered to have a "deficiency state" of any of them, as you may if you become depleted enough of the basic vitamins and minerals. This is not to say, however, that a selection of some of these preparations may not prove to be essential to your maintenance of good health or your return to good health. However, choosing the right ones is not always straightforward, and no single regimen of supplementation is right for everyone. Let's look at each of these categories in more depth.

MINERALS: A MAZE OF CONFUSION

Remember that minerals are nonorganic substances, containing the elements essential for survival in nonorganic forms not generally appropriate for direct human ingestion. With a few notable exceptions, nonorganic substances are designed primarily for the support of plant life, while organic substances are designed primarily for the support of animal and human life. Simply put, an example of a nonorganic substance would be a rock, and an example of an organic substance would be an apple. Common sense tells us that we can directly consume only the apple. However, plants can take rock-based minerals and eventually process them into an organic form that will nourish the body. So although we cannot eat the rock directly, we can eat the plant that was partially nourished by the rock-based minerals.

The difference between inorganic and organic forms of essential elements is addressed by the concept of *bioavailability*. Bioavailability is NOT the same thing as absorbability. Many inorganic forms of ionic elements (for example, the magnesium in magnesium oxide and the calcium in calcium carbonate) are easily absorbed from the digestive tract into the bloodstream. However, *absorption* from the digestive tract does not assure *delivery* to the proper target sites in the proper target tissues. Nor does it assure that delivery will not be made to the wrong tissues. Many ionic element forms must be delivered to the body in organic, foodlike forms to assure delivery to the proper tissues.

Although it is not a mineral, vitamin D provides a good example of this delivery concept. When sunlight forms active vitamin D (cholecalciferol) in the skin, a specific blood protein attaches to the vitamin and carries it to target tissues. When the tissue receptor sites are physically near, the blood protein will release its attachment to the nutrient and allow its efficient binding to the receptor sites. This mechanism not only allows a very efficient delivery of a nutrient to the precise location where it is needed, but also minimizes the need to "overdose" the body with that nutrient to assure that it gets where it needs to go. This naturally efficient form of nutrient delivery also makes it much less likely that a nutrient will overaccumulate in the wrong place.

While all vitamins and minerals have not had specific blood transport proteins identified for them, variations in how different foods are digested also help to determine how a nutrient is released into the blood to find its target tissues. Many digestive processes deliver vitamin and mineral nutrients into the blood very slowly and in association with other food molecules absorbed at the same time. Never be fooled into thinking that any supplement that is easily absorbed is also a supplement that must be bioavailable as well. Remember that Mother Nature never intended for you to eat a rock, whether it is packaged as an easily swallowable pill or not. As we shall see later, such a supplement is actually toxic, further separating you from the good health that you are trying to attain. You would hope that taking any commercially produced supplement would do at least some good for you, but this is not necessarily the case.

Another reason why the concept of bioavailability is different from the concept of absorbability has to do with the rates of dissociation and reassociation seen with different mineral preparations. Anything that can be dissolved also has a tendency to precipitate and drop back out of solution into its predissolved, solid form. Just because something can ionize and go into solution doesn't mean it will stay in solution. Any dissolved substance can reassociate or recomplex together, and drop back out of solution. Highly dissolvable substances have weak ionic charges holding the substance together, tending to let them stay dissolved. However, other substances have strong ionic charges that can readily result in a recomplexing that will cause the dissolved substance to again drop out of solution. If a dissolved rock that was absorbed into the bloodstream later reassociates and deposits inside your tissues, it's easy to understand why your health might be severely compromised by the chronic ingestion of such a substance.

Calcium carbonate is the mineral form of calcium that is the predominant form in dolomite, a very common and cheap source of calcium used in many supplement preparations today. One of the primary characteristics of calcium carbonate in nature is its tendency to precipitate out of solution back into its hard, rocklike form. Stalactites and stalagmites, the spears of rock on the ground and hanging from the ceilings in caves, are dramatic examples of this precipitation. In nature, this precipitation occurs when the water content of the dissolved calcium carbonate begins to evaporate, concentrating the mineral and making it easier for it to drop out of solution.

In the body, similar factors can promote the undesirable precipitation of poorly dissociated mineral forms out of the blood, including this very same calcium carbonate just mentioned. Dehydration, whether caused by the failure to drink enough water or by taking medications such as diuretics, can promote this precipitation. The concentrations and numbers of other solutes, or dissolved substances, in the blood can also affect this tendency to precipitate.

The blood does not have an unlimited capacity to absorb new solutes. When too much of a new substance is absorbed, something else has to precipitate out. One's general health status also affects precipitation. When the acid–base balance of the blood gets out of whack, precipitation may increase. Also, after the precipitation process has already started in the tissues, just as with the calcium deposits seen in the atherosclerotic hardening of the arteries, it is easier for new precipitation to "attach" to the old sites of precipitation and drop out of solution. Just like the stalactites and the stalagmites, once the process has been initiated, it takes much less precipitating "pressure" to continue the process. Many processes in chemistry and biology are much easier to continue than to initiate.

Precipitation can also occur when you take large dosages of supplementation. Even a highly dissolvable form of calcium with weak ionic attractions when dissolved, such as calcium chloride or calcium citrate, will eventually saturate the blood and drop out of solution in combination with a variety of other negatively charged dissolved particles, or anions. So even if your calcium (or other mineral element) doesn't come from a rock, it can still eventually deposit abnormally in your tissues if you take too much. There is a lot of calcium in most diets, and even a relatively small amount of calcium supplementation taken on a regular basis can result in undesirable, rocklike, nonbiologic deposits of calcium in the tissues. These calcium deposits will promote and accelerate almost all of the many different degenerative diseases seen with increasing age. Short-term calcium supplementation to support bone healing and healing in general is about the only reasonable way to supplement this mineral element. Toxicity and poor nutrition are the primary causes of osteoporosis, and these factors must first be addressed if osteoporosis is to be controlled. Causing other diseases with indiscriminate calcium supplementation is not the answer to trying to protect yourself from osteoporosis.

Let's look at one horrifying example of the form many minerals take in supplementation and in foods touted to be enriched. A television station in Denver once aired a children's scientific program, aiming to reassure the children and adult viewers that their breakfast cereal was full of healthy minerals, while giving them an enjoyable lesson in magnetism. When enriched cornflakes were placed on milk, a strong magnet was actually able to steer a flake around on top of the milk! These cornflakes were advertised as containing 100 percent or more of the recommended daily allowances for most of the vitamins and minerals. What was demonstrated next should upset and even infuriate most of you. Using a plastic bag, a large portion of the cornflakes was mixed with water until a reasonably uniform slurry was formed. Then a strong magnet was applied to the outside of the bag and the slurry was sloshed back and forth across the magnet. After only a few seconds, a clear accumulation of *iron filings* was clinging to the magnet through the plastic bag! If this is a bioavailable, organic, nutritious form of iron, then you should be able to just grind a nail with a file on top of your cereal for your next breakfast, just like the Parmesan cheese is ground onto your pasta.

There are really three unsettling questions that pose themselves from this demonstration. First, where in the body is all that metallic iron accumulating? Second, do the producers of the show really think metallic iron is a good thing to eat? And third, what forms do most of the other vitamins and minerals take in other "enriched" foods? The supplementation of metallic iron can be detected by a strong magnet, but the other toxic supplement forms cannot be similarly pulled out of the cereal soup in this demonstration and also be properly exposed. When you realize that these inorganic, inedible forms of common minerals are the cheapest to produce and to add to foods, you should seriously consider never eating an "enriched" food again. Eat fresh foods as close to their natural state as possible, and supplement their deficiencies intelligently in the fashion discussed later in this chapter.

Many mineral preparations advertise their products as being highly absorbable. At first blush, this might seem to be highly desirable. However, few mineral elements are needed in large amounts, and most are only required in the most tiny, infinitesimal amounts. Even the most severely mineral-depleted individual does not need, amount-wise, the quantities of minerals that are in most preparations.

Many supplement manufacturers claim good clinical results with their preparations. And many of these claims are probably true, but only when viewed in the short term. A person who is literally starving to death can be kept alive, and even temporarily restored to *relatively* good health, by virtually any kind of food. This does not mean that the starvation diet will sustain or promote good health if it is eaten indefinitely on a regular basis. Similarly, a mineral-depleted individual can initially show a good clinical response when "flooded" with a nonorganic source of minerals, but the benefit will only be short-lived. In the long run, a toxic effect can be expected to develop. These ionic element forms can literally recharge many of the body's important enzyme and cellular functions and in so doing acutely improve health, while at the same time they are massively accumulating in other tissues where they are not required.

When you fill a storage area with one item unintentionally, you can no longer put the other desirable items into storage there. The situation is no different with the body. Overdoses of nonorganically based elements seen in many mineral preparations must accumulate when they are continually taken, and the result is usually bad in the long run. Even though much of the excess will be naturally eliminated, an eventual accumulation is nevertheless inevitable. This accumulation will have its own toxic effect, keeping the tissues from functioning properly and preventing the accumulation of other valuable nutrients that should be present.

One of the best examples of this toxic accumulation is seen with the most common forms of calcium supplementation. The dairy industry and the osteoporosis experts have convinced the public that massively supplemented calcium is essential to good health and strong bones. In fact, calcium is available in a wide variety of foods. Although you can still become depleted of calcium in your bones with all the calcium available in foods, the real reasons for calcium depletion have more to do with toxins and the chronic ingestion of calcium-mobilizing foods than with the actual lack of calcium in the diet.

Toxins, especially those of dental origin, disrupt the calcium–phosphorus balance, causing a continual mobilization of calcium out of the bones and into the urine. Also, sugar, caffeine, and soft drinks, three of the most commonly eaten substances, all directly promote this increased urinary excretion of calcium mobilized from the bones. In most people, the calcium present in the diet cannot keep pace with this ongoing mobilization, and osteoporosis of some degree is inevitable if you get old enough.

Hair analysis studies done on patients before they had their dental toxins removed revealed an interesting finding. Calcium levels in the hair were typically elevated in most of these patients. This finding is consistent with the continual mobilization of calcium, first into the blood and then into the urine, by toxins and persistently poor food choices. It is also consistent with the regular dairy intake and calcium supplementation typical of many of those patients. However, patients aged seventy or older almost always had normal or even slightly low hair calcium levels. It appeared that patients with chronic and significant elevations of calcium in their hair simply did not live to grow old.

This observation has received some unintended support from the recent scientific literature. Zhang et al. published research that showed that women with *higher* bone mass were at higher risk for postmenopausal breast cancer.[1] Lucas et al. and Cauley et al. reached the same conclusion.[2,3] Probably the one thing that all of these women had in common was the long-term ingestion of calcium supplements, usually of rock or other nonorganic origin. Massive amounts of calcium from such sources will increase bone density only slightly, while significantly increasing unwanted calcium deposition elsewhere in the body. Such deposits of calcium will not only increase hair levels of calcium, they will also promote degenerative diseases of all kinds, of which breast cancer is only one. In fact, Evans et al. published that most of the fifty women with one kind of breast cancer (ductal carcinoma in situ) had calcifications on their mammograms.[4] Furthermore, Curhan et al. demonstrated that high *supplemental* calcium may *increase* the risk of symptomatic kidney stones, while high *dietary* calcium intake appears to *decrease* this risk.[5] This epidemic of calcium supplementation is also probably one of the major contributing factors to heart attack, a condition almost always associated with calcification of the blood vessels supplying the heart.

Should anyone be taking calcium supplements? In my opinion, absolutely not. Except in those rare cases where supplemental calcium is needed on a short-term basis to promote healing from an injury, calcium supplements should be avoided, even if they do come from a bioavailable source. Calcium is easily overdosed, and the effects of its overaccumulation are certainly at least as undesirable as an osteoporotic fracture. Most people would prefer to have a *slightly* greater chance of such a fracture than a *significantly* greater chance of heart attack, cancer, or some other debilitating and life-threatening degenerative disease.

Of course, the real solution to the ravages of osteoporosis is proper nutrition and proper removal of toxins, aiming to prevent or postpone the condition from happening, or to slow or stop its pro-gression. And even if you already have advanced osteoporosis from a lifetime of toxicity and poor foods, it makes no sense to increase your predisposition to so many other diseases to achieve the slight decrease in the risk of fracture that you *might* get from massive cal-cium supplementation.

BASIC SUPPLEMENT FORMS

The basic forms of mineral element supplements come as inorganic forms, colloidal forms, and organic chelated forms. I recommend that you use the organic chelated forms for the following reasons.

INORGANIC MINERALS

The inorganic forms are typified by the calcium supplements de-rived from dolomite. Dolomite is actually a rock, and ingesting it in any form, even if ground to powder in a tablet, will prove to be far more toxic than beneficial. Inorganic forms of mineral elements, as a *general* rule, are present in large, high-milligram amounts in the cheaper supplement preparations.

Only a few of the very common elements, such as ionic sodium, potassium, and chloride, can be routinely ingested as simple in-organic salts. Sodium chloride, or common table salt, is a good example of such a formulation. The body requires these elements in very large amounts. Because of this, it is difficult (but not impossible) to overdose on them, as can easily occur with other highly absorbable inorganic salt forms of the mineral elements. This is one reason why taking sea salt is not such a wonderful idea. Sea salt presents most of its mineral elements in the inorganic simple salt form. These elements are absorbed very readily, but they are not associated with the carrier food molecules that allow the effective delivery of small quantities of these elements to the target tissues and target cellular sites. Furthermore, sea salt contains trace to small amounts of many of the highly toxic heavy metals. Having a purely "natural" source of mineral elements is no guarantee that the equally "natural" toxic heavy metals are not also present.

Colloidal Minerals

Colloidal forms of mineral elements are becoming increasingly popular. These forms are advertised as being highly absorbable. However, high absorbability does not assure bioavailability. As I mentioned earlier, high doses of highly absorbed minerals can easily become overdoses in the long run. And an overdose is as undesirable as a deficiency. Furthermore, many of the colloidal forms come from inorganic sources, such as clay. Like a ground-up rock, clay also bears little resemblance to the food forms of the mineral elements. And like the example of sea salt mentioned in the paragraph above, most sources of a wide variety of minerals that come directly from the earth's crust will have desirable mineral elements as well as a variety of undesirable toxic heavy metals. Even if such toxins are present in tiny amounts, they will accumulate in the body over time, and a toxic effect can be expected to emerge after the early honeymoon period of improvement.

There is another form of colloidal supplementation that claims to overcome the shortcomings of the inorganically based colloidal minerals, such as are derived from clay. These supplements are touted as coming from "plant" sources, but typically from ancient plants. First of all, ancient plants are not the same as having a fresh plant or vegetable food source. The molecules that supply bioavailability versus mere absorption would not predominate in such a preparation. If the ancient plant source is no longer directly edible, it is doubtful that any significant bioavailability remains. Furthermore, many of the plant-based colloidal preparations, like the inorganically based colloidal preparations, contain small amounts of toxic mineral elements. In fact, in the plant-based colloidal forms, these toxic elements are sometimes even more pronounced.

Algae, a plant form that is the source for some of the organic colloidal mineral forms, works with microbes to actively remove toxic metals and other organic chemicals from its surrounding environment, working as a toxin concentrator. It only makes good sense to get your bioavailable minerals with as few associated toxins as possible. It doesn't make sense to deliberately introduce *any* amount of toxic heavy metals into your body, no matter how small that amount is.

CHELATED MINERALS

The organic chelated forms of the mineral elements remain your best choices for routine supplementation. These forms present to the digestive tract attached to a variety of different molecules. These companion molecules can include amino acids, small proteins (multiple amino acids complexed together), or other molecules commonly encountered in the natural breakdown of food being digested. In contrast to the inorganic rock-based forms of the mineral elements, organic chelated elements will be present in supplements in very small amounts, and the preparations that contain them will tend to be costlier. Remember, food costs more than rocks.

When you examine a bottle of supplemental minerals, look for the term *chelated,* and note whether the label specifies that the mineral is bound to amino acids, proteinates, carbohydrates, or other foodlike forms. For example, some labels might say "zinc (chelate)." This means a form of zinc that is bound to an amino acid. Others might just specify "boron (chelate)," if the boron is bound to something other than an amino acid. Sometimes the label may be more specific. It might say, for example, that the product contains selenium as selenomethionine, which is selenium bound to the amino acid methionine. It's also not a bad idea to get at least some of your supplemental minerals as ascorbate (for example, as magnesium ascorbate), which delivers the mineral with vitamin C.

The milligram or microgram amounts of chelated minerals may be so low in these preparations that you feel you aren't getting your money's worth. But remember that your body requires only *small* amounts of *bioavailable* mineral forms on a regular basis. High doses of the more poorly absorbed inorganic mineral forms are never desirable.

Don't be afraid to ask specific questions of whatever company you choose as a supplier of your supplemental needs.

MINERALS

The common minerals present in the body in large amounts (macrominerals) include the following:

1. *Calcium.* Vital for the proper function of all cells; also essential for proper bone formation and maintenance. Supplementation not generally recommended, except to acutely support healing. Even in the presence of osteoporosis, calcium supplementation has strong counterbalancing negatives, promoting most other degenerative diseases, including cancer and heart disease.

Common dietary sources: sardines, clams and oysters; turnip greens, mustard greens, broccoli, peas, beans; fruits. Note that pasteurized milk and milk products, fortified with vitamin D, deliver too much calcium to tissues other than the bones, promoting degenerative diseases.

2. *Chloride.* Major cellular anion, maintaining pH balance, activating enzymes, and essential for the formation of hydrochloric acid in the stomach. Except for using sodium chloride (table salt) to taste, no specific supplementation is required.

   Common dietary sources: table salt, seafood, meat, eggs.

3. *Magnesium.* Vital for bone formation. Essential for activating many different enzymes; involved in protein synthesis and nerve impulse transmission. When a magnesium deficiency exists, bioavailable magnesium supplementation can increase bone mass. Consider supplementing with 20 to 100 milligrams of a properly chelated form. Higher doses can be used temporarily to help mobilize excess accumulations of calcium in the body as reflected on hair analysis.

   Common dietary sources: nuts, peas, beans, cereal grains, corn, carrots, seafood, brown rice, parsley, spinach.

4. *Phosphorus.* Companion mineral to calcium; activator of many different enzymes. Generally should not be supplemented, for the same reasons as calcium.

   Common dietary sources: meat, poultry, fish, eggs, nuts, peas, beans, grains.

5. *Potassium.* Important cellular electrolyte; integrally involved with calcium and sodium in proper cell membrane function. Consider supplementing when blood or hair levels are low, but only with proper follow-up of subsequent blood and hair levels with a competent health care practitioner.

   Common dietary sources: avocado, fruits, potatoes, beans, tomato, wheat bran, eggs.

6. *Sodium.* Important cellular electrolyte, along with calcium and potassium. Generally needs only to be supplemented as table salt to taste.
   Common dietary sources: table salt, meat, seafood, vegetables.
7. *Sulfur.* Important component of some amino acids. Consider supplementation only with organic forms such as MSM.
   Common dietary sources: high-protein foods such as meat, poultry, fish, eggs, peas, nuts, beans.

The common minerals present in the body in small or trace amounts (microminerals) include the following:

1. *Boron.* Important for maintaining bone strength and structure. Consider supplementing with 100 to 200 micrograms daily of a chelated form.
   Common dietary sources: fruits, vegetables, peas, beans, nuts.
2. *Chromium.* Important for the proper interaction of insulin and blood glucose. Consider supplementing with 25 to 50 micrograms daily of a chelated form.
   Common dietary sources: prunes, nuts, asparagus, organ meats, grains.
3. *Copper.* Required for the proper use of iron by the body. Easy to overdose and hard to be frankly deficient. In general, avoid supplementing with copper; if supplementation is taken, be certain that the copper is in a chelated form, take no more than 1 milligram daily, and regularly reevaluate the need for ongoing supplementation.
   Common dietary sources: liver, seafood (especially shellfish), grains, peas, beans, nuts, eggs, meats, poultry.
4. *Iodine.* Required for thyroid hormone synthesis. Consider supplementing with 150 micrograms daily of a form such as potassium iodide.

Common dietary sources: iodized salt, saltwater seafood, eggs, beef liver, peanuts, spinach, pumpkin, broccoli.

5. *Iron.* Required for the synthesis of red blood cells. Generally, men and postmenopausal women should never supplement iron, since it can easily accumulate to toxic levels in the absence of loss by bleeding. Menstruating women should consider supplementing under the guidance of a health care practitioner.
   Common dietary sources: meat, especially organ meats such as liver; clams and oysters; peas, beans, nuts, seeds, green leafy vegetables, fruits, grains.

6. *Manganese.* Important for normal brain function and numerous enzyme systems. Consider supplementing with 2 to 4 milligrams daily of a chelated form.
   Common dietary sources: wheat bran, peas, beans, nuts, lettuce, blueberries, pineapple, seafood, poultry, meat.

7. *Molybdenum.* Important for the metabolism of the building blocks of DNA and RNA. Consider supplementing with 10 to 20 micrograms daily of a chelated form.
   Common dietary sources: soybeans, lentils, buckwheat, oats, rice.

8. *Selenium.* Protects cells against free radicals; also helps neutralize heavy metals such as mercury. Consider supplementing with 10 to 20 micrograms daily of a chelated form. Men with higher levels of selenium appear to have a lower risk of prostate cancer than men with lower levels.
   Common dietary sources: grains, meats, poultry, fish.

9. *Zinc.* Important for energy metabolism and the function of many enzymatic systems. Consider supplementing with 5 to 15 milligrams daily of a chelated form.
   Common dietary sources: oysters, wheat germ, beef liver, dark poultry meats, grains.

Finally, don't take a large variety of different supplements each of which contains several vitamins or minerals. You can easily exceed the recommended dosages. Many preparations include various other nutrients along with the "featured" nutrient. Do your arithmetic, and don't overdo it!

VITAMINS

Unlike most minerals, vitamins are already in an organic form. This is not to say that all purified vitamins are in as bioavailable a form as they are in foods. However, a purified vitamin will be much closer to a food form than most minerals as found in the earth's crust. Having noted this distinction, it is nevertheless important to also find vitamins in forms as close to food forms as possible.

Many vitamins can be overdosed relatively easily. The main reason for this is that vitamins, while vital to proper bodily function, are needed in only the tiniest of amounts, as a general rule. When dealing with supplementation of any kind, you simply cannot assume that if a little is good, more must be better. Always remember that EVERYTHING is toxic in a high enough dose. No exceptions. And this includes many things that your body requires for survival. Everything in the biological sciences needs balance, and too much of something good should be avoided just as diligently as too little of it.

Vitamins comprise a very diverse group of organic substances. For the most part, these substances are not related at all in their chemical structures or physiological roles. Nevertheless, they are divided into two broad categories, based on how they are absorbed into the body: water-soluble vitamins and fat-soluble vitamins.

There are four fat-soluble vitamins:

1. *Vitamin A.* Essential for vision, for the immune system, and for functions associated with proper growth; also an antioxi-

dant. Probably best supplemented as beta-carotene, which converts to vitamin A and minimizes the possibility of overdosage. Melhus et al. have shown that too much vitamin A is associated with reduced bone mineral density and increased risk for hip fracture.[6]

Common dietary sources: beef liver, sweet potatoes, carrots, spinach, butternut squash.

2. *Vitamin D.* Essential for good skeletal growth and strong bones. Only minimal exposure to sunlight is necessary to meet the daily requirement. Vitamin D is easily overdosed and can promote abnormal calcification throughout the body, since it increases calcium absorption from the gut; the increased calcium absorbed does not necessarily seek out the bones, however. Schwartzman and Franck demonstrated that pharmacological doses of vitamin D will *worsen* osteoporosis.[7] Consider not supplementing this vitamin at all, unless you do so in close coordination with your health care provider, making sure that the desired clinical effects are being accomplished.

   Common dietary sources: few natural dietary sources; present in fortified milk, but this is not recommended.

3. *Vitamin E.* Helps to maintain the integrity of cell membranes; also an antioxidant. Try to take preparations with as much d-alpha-tocopherol content as possible. In general, do not exceed 800 IU per day; 400 IU per day would probably be advisable for most.

   Common dietary sources: vegetable seed oils, peanuts. Lesser amounts in many different fresh vegetables and fruits.

4. *Vitamin K.* Necessary for proper blood clotting. Does not generally need supplementation unless some form of malabsorption exists in the gut, or if the bacteria in the gut that manufacture this vitamin have been destroyed.

   Common dietary sources: green leafy vegetables, soybeans, beef liver.

Rapola et al. found that beta-carotene significantly increased the number of fatal heart attacks among men with previous heart attack who smoked.[8] Without a good explanation of why this effect has been observed, it would be safest to advise smoking patients who have known heart disease to avoid beta-carotene and other vitamin A supplementation completely for the time being. However, an epidemiological study suggests that a diet rich in beta-carotene may lower a woman's risk of breast cancer after menopause, so a complete avoidance of beta-carotene supplementation for everyone is certainly not being recommended at this time.[9] Further research may be needed to determine if supplemented beta-carotene is significantly less desirable than dietary beta-carotene. Certainly, as a general rule, supplemented nutrients can never be as desirable as dietary nutrients.

The fat-soluble vitamins are absorbed along with dietary fats. Normally, these vitamins are not excreted in the urine, but are stored in the body in moderate amounts. Conversely, the water-soluble vitamins are more numerous, are excreted in the urine, and are not stored in the body in appreciable quantities. Most authorities consider that there are nine water-soluble vitamins:

1. *Vitamin B_1 (thiamin).* Helps to generate cellular energy, promote fatty acid synthesis, and support normal membrane and nerve conduction. Little toxicity has been observed with high oral intakes; unless a deficiency exists, consider supplementing with 5 to 25 milligrams daily.
   Common dietary sources: yeast, sunflower seeds, peas, beans.
2. *Vitamin B_2 (riboflavin).* Important for the cellular reactions that transfer energy from one chemical substance to another; also serves as an antioxidant; helps in the formation of energy from food fats and proteins. Deficiency syndrome has not been clearly characterized; consider supplementing with 5 to 15 milligrams daily.

Common dietary sources: beef liver, meat, oysters.

3. *Vitamin B$_3$ (niacin).* Important for the proper function of numerous enzymes and of the brain and nervous system; important for the synthesis of many hormones. Deficiency causes a syndrome called pellagra. A supplement of 5 to 20 milligrams daily is probably acceptable for most people. Niacin can excessively accelerate detoxification in susceptible individuals, especially in those who have their dental toxicity removed.
   Common dietary sources: beef and beef liver, poultry, fish.

4. *Vitamin B$_6$ (pyridoxine).* Important for the proper function of many enzymes involved in amino acid metabolism. Consider supplementing with 5 to 15 milligrams daily.
   Common dietary sources: meat, beans, potatoes, bananas.

5. *Folic acid.* Important for the synthesis of DNA and for the metabolism of amino acids and histidine. Consider supplementing with 200 to 400 micrograms daily.
   Common dietary sources: brewer's yeast, spinach, asparagus, turnip greens, lima beans, beef liver.

6. *Vitamin C (ascorbic acid).* Believed to be important for fat metabolism, immune function and healing, endocrine function, and neutralization of toxicity; also an antioxidant. Important to take adequate doses on a regular basis; many individuals will do best on 10 to 15 grams of sodium ascorbate daily, taken under the direction of their health care provider.
   Common dietary sources: papaya, orange, cantaloupe, broccoli, brussels sprouts, green peppers, grapefruit, strawberries.

7. *Vitamin B$_{12}$ (cobalamine).* Important for the maintenance of proper nerve function and blood synthesis. Unless a clear deficiency syndrome exists (pernicious anemia and/or markedly low blood levels of the vitamin), consider avoiding any supplementation, since supplement forms of B$_{12}$

can promote the methylation of inorganic mercury in the body, making it much more toxic and causing clinical compromise.

Common dietary sources: meat, seafood, poultry.

8. *Biotin.* Important for energy metabolism. Consider supplementing with 100 to 200 micrograms daily.

   Common dietary sources: yeast, liver, kidney.

9. *Pantothenic acid.* A precursor to the body's synthesis of its own coenzyme A; important for the metabolism of carbohydrates and fats. Consider supplementing with 10 to 20 milligrams daily.

   Common dietary sources: widespread; especially high in egg yolk, liver, kidney, yeast.

VITAMIN C

Vitamin C is such an important supplement that it deserves its own special section. Vitamin C is usually supplemented in one of three forms: ascorbic acid, calcium ascorbate, or sodium ascorbate. The ascorbate anion can be supplemented as part of many different mineral chelates, but these three forms are the major sources of supplemented vitamin C.

In the amounts that I recommend, the best form of vitamin C to take is sodium ascorbate. Calcium ascorbate supplies too much calcium, which is undesirable for reasons that I explained earlier. Ascorbic acid can impair digestion by decreasing enzyme and acid production in the stomach when it is taken close to a meal. It can also erode tooth enamel if it is frequently in contact with the tooth surfaces.

Except when taking only a couple of grams (1 gram = 1,000 milligrams) or less of vitamin C, the preparations that add rutin and other bioflavonoids should be avoided. Megadoses of vitamin C are being promoted here, but the effects of megadose rutin and other bioflavonoids, compounds felt by some to enhance the effects of vitamin C, are unknown.

You may be concerned about taking in too much sodium if you take megadoses of sodium ascorbate. After all, doesn't sodium raise the blood pressure and make high blood pressure (hypertension) even more difficult to control? Actually, I have never observed this problem in any patient to whom I have given sodium ascorbate by mouth or vein. In fact, some very good clinical research indicates that it is the chloride in common table salt, not simply the sodium, that elevates blood pressure. But sodium and table salt have come to be considered the same substance, even though this is not true. Sodium is only a part of table salt, not the entire compound. Kurtz et al. showed that sodium *chloride* raised the blood pressure of men with high blood pressure, while sodium *citrate* did not.[10] Kurtz and Morris also showed in animal studies that sodium expanded plasma volume and elevated blood pressure only when it was given as sodium chloride.[11] Neither the blood volume nor the blood pressure was increased when sodium was given with bicarbonate, phosphate, glutamate, glycinate, aspartate, or ascorbate (vitamin C). The time-honored concept of "sodium-dependent" hypertension needs to be replaced by a new concept of "sodium chloride–dependent" hypertension.

Vitamin C is one of the few supplements that are extremely difficult to overdose. Whether administered orally or intravenously, megadose vitamin C has been shown to be a superlative therapy for heavy-metal poisoning; carbon monoxide exposure and poisoning; pesticide exposure; allergic and toxic shock from snakebite or insect bite; and almost all viral diseases studied, including polio, hepatitis, and herpes. Frederick Klenner, M.D., published much of the significant work documenting these marvelous effects of megadose vitamin C.[12–15] In many of the conditions listed above, Dr. Klenner would often report clinical cures, with return of blood tests to normal, after only a few days of therapy. However, the doses that he used, typically as sodium ascorbate administered intravenously, ranged from a few grams to a few *hundred* grams daily. No other modern study on vitamin C even approaches these doses, so Dr. Klenner's work still constitutes the only substantial published documentation of the effects of such very large doses.

Although Dr. Klenner's findings serve notice of the enormous utility of intravenous vitamin C, most people are not going to take an IV on a daily, or even a weekly, basis. However, for patients seeking a therapy to help neutralize toxicity and give their struggling immune systems a chance to recover, frequent 40- to 60-gram infusions of vitamin C can help achieve just that.

The more common way to take vitamin C is orally. Doses of 10 to 15 grams daily are advisable for most people, in my opinion. This would amount to a heaping teaspoon of sodium ascorbate taken twice daily in water or dilute juice. However, oral vitamin C will very quickly let you know when you have taken too much of it. Too much vitamin C will cause a loose diarrhea, usually lasting for a few hours. Some people will get diarrhea before they reach the recommended 10 grams, while many others won't get it until they reach 40 grams or more. For those who want further information on this topic, Cathcart published a method for determining the optimal dosage of vitamin C in different diseases based on bowel tolerance (that is, the point at which diarrhea begins).[16]

Once you have experimented a bit with oral sodium ascorbate to find out how much it takes to cause diarrhea, you can take *just short* of that dose on a daily basis, even if it is more than 15 grams. This will have a beneficial effect on your general health. When you decrease your bowel transit time with oral vitamin C, you can keep your colon fairly clear of feces most of the time. This accelerated emptying of the gut and colon can substantially decrease the toxicity that most of us face on a daily basis from poorly digested food, for reasons that I explained at length in chapter 2. Not only will shorter bowel transit time facilitate the elimination of toxins, but direct contact with vitamin C will directly neutralize much of the bacterial toxicity in your gut before it gets absorbed. The direct contact with the vitamin C will inactivate or neutralize most bacterial toxins while facilitating their direct elimination with the shorter bowel transit time induced by the vitamin C. Of course, the high doses of oral vitamin C also allow the optimal absorption of vitamin C into the blood, where daily toxicity from all sources can also be neutralized as it appears in the blood. Periodically, for all of these reasons, it's also a good idea to take a "C-flush," taking enough vitamin C to deliberately induce this cleansing diarrhea. This is best done when you are not working and have easy access to a toilet. To minimize the buildup of uncomfortable gas, take a little powdered activated charcoal with the vitamin C. It is also extremely important to drink large amounts of water to prevent your body from becoming dehydrated once the diarrhea starts. For those who have schedules that can deal with the inconvenience of the self-limited diarrhea, doing a "C-flush" on a daily basis can be a very healthy habit.

Some medical authorities continue to advise against megadose vitamin C therapy, claiming that it increases the incidence of kidney stones and the potential for kidney failure. With the use of sodium ascorbate as the primary source of vitamin C, these concerns just do not seem to be justified. In fact, the ability of vitamin C to neutralize so many different toxins appears to benefit those with kidney disease as well. However, large doses of vitamin C should probably be avoided if you drink very little water. Optimal hydration is important in general, but you should avoid high doses of vitamin C (or anything else, for that matter) if you are chronically dehydrated.

OTHER SOURCES OF NUTRIENTS

One good way to get a variety of bioavailable vitamins and minerals is to look to a number of different foodstuffs that naturally concentrate them. For those who aren't allergic, bee pollen is a rich source of many different vitamins, minerals, and proteins.

Unpolished brown rice that has not been stripped down to the largely nutrient-free polished white rice is a rich source of vitamin B_1. There are also different grain germs (wheat germ, for example), which contain most of the nutrient value of the grains from which they were stripped. You can cook with these or add them back to your cereals. Brewer's yeast (as distinguished from baker's yeast) can be an excellent source of vitamins, minerals, and amino acids.

These are but a few of the natural nutrient sources that can become a regular part of your diet. Using these natural nutrient sources also makes it very difficult to ever overdose on a particular nutrient. But, as with everything else, any of the nutrient sources can be overdone if you don't practice moderation. Don't try to get most of your nutrients from just a few sources. Try to keep your diet as diverse as possible. If you eat strictly according to taste, you will still be prone to nutrient depletion, even if the foods you do eat are high quality and fresh.

Occasionally, you may need to take amino acid supplements. In general, if your diet is balanced and your digestion is proceeding efficiently, you won't need to supplement amino acids. You should really only consider taking this kind of supplementation when your laboratory studies indicate that you are having difficulty in maintaining proper protein synthesis and balance. Generally, this will occur in the context of persistently poor digestion and inadequate assimilation of the protein building blocks from the food.

Should you decide to supplement amino acids, be sure to take them in as much of a balance as possible. Take an amino acid supplement that has all of the amino acids, not just a few that you may consider to be the most important. And if you think that imbalanced amino acids couldn't possibly do you any harm, look at the example of the sweetener aspartame. Aspartame is an artificial sweetener that consists primarily of two amino acids, phenylalanine and aspartic acid. These two amino acids accumulate out of control in heavy users, giving rise to a wide variety of negative side effects, especially neurologic side effects. (Other reasons to avoid aspartame are given in chapter 3.) Amino acids need other amino acids to synthesize protein. In general, taking just a few can allow for an abnormal accumulation.

JUICING

Juicing is another dietary habit that requires moderation. Certainly any fruit or vegetable juice is far better for you than a soft drink or some other sugar-laced beverage. But the principle of moderation must once again be heeded. Juicing allows you to eat far more vegetables or fruit than you possibly could eat if you were to eat them whole. Nature has a way of determining your need for a food based on your hunger or appetite. Don't chronically "trick" your body into eating far more nutrient substances than it possibly could under normal circumstances. Undesirable mineral balances can result from a preoccupation with juicing. Have one small glass of juice or less each day; don't let juice become the entire focus of your diet. This is not to say, however, that some regular juicing cannot be a very valuable addition to your diet. Your clinical status, as well as your bloodwork and hair analysis, can give added clues as to whether you are drinking too much juice.

UNDERSTANDING LABELS

Also beware of the many supplements labeled as containing "natural ingredients." Taken to the extreme, and such labeling often is, just about any substance can be termed a "natural" ingredient, or termed as being derived from a natural substance. Remember that nature has many toxic substances that exist in nature, side by side with its many nutritious substances. Given the imprecision with which this term is currently used, mercury and lead could be considered natural ingredients in certain contexts. To make matters worse, if an ingredient can be classified as "natural" within certain parameters, it doesn't even have to be listed among the contents on the label.

The Food and Drug Administration actually has an insect that is approved for consumption. The cochineal insect, harvested in Peru and the Canary Islands, brings the bright red color to many of the foods and drinks commercially sold. Containing carmine, to which some people can have life-threatening allergic reactions, such products are rarely ever listed on the label. Carmine is considered a "natural" color, so a company is not required to list it on the label.

Labels can also be misleading when they list subproducts. Many foods contain products that contain other substances that are not listed separately. A label for commercial spaghetti sauce might not list sugar or one of its many synonyms on the label, but it might list tomato paste—and tomato paste contains sugar.

All of this means that a commercial product that doesn't list sugar, or carmine, or something else you want to avoid could still contain significant amounts of that substance. Buyer beware. Or perhaps more accurately: Buyer, be aware!

SPECIAL SUPPLEMENTS

Although this section is not intended to be all-inclusive, a few particular supplements should be especially noted. Although some of these supplements may also contain some vitamins and minerals, they are not specifically intended to be only vitamin and/or mineral supplements. In general, it is usually desirable to take a supplement that has a relatively unique manner of supporting or improving immune function. Since it is impossible to take all of the supplements available today, it is intelligent to take a variety of supplements that support immune function in as many different ways as possible. When trying to decide which of these supplements should be taken, always follow the suggestions given below to make sure you are experiencing a clinical benefit, rather than possibly causing too rapid a detoxification, which can hurt your health. Trial-and-error often ends up being the most effective way of determining what's best for you. What works great for someone else might actually make you ill.

COLOSTRUM

Colostrum supplements are now commercially available. Colostrum is the "first milk" of a lactating mammal. The commercial preparations presently only use the colostrum of nursing cows. It is important to note that colostrum is not really milk at all, even though it comes down the same channels in the udder that later deliver the milk. In addition to having significant amounts of bioavailable vitamins and minerals, colostrum also has unique immune system–supporting growth factors. Interestingly, some of the most important of these factors are not species-specific to only the cow; they are identical to the same factors in colostrum of human origin.

Colostrum contains many different substances that directly affect immune function. This is perhaps the most important reason for its therapeutic effects. One especially potent and well-studied immune factor found in colostrum is a substance called transfer factor. Transfer factor harvested from a healthy person is known to "transfer" much of the immune competence of the healthy donor to a needy, immunocompromised patient. Colostrum makes this process much simpler.

Colostrum can be taken regularly, or it can be reserved for times when you feel that you are facing particularly strong stresses on your immune system. Generally, colostrum has not been observed to stimulate detoxification faster than the strengthened immune system can neutralize the released toxins. However, this balance between detoxification rate and the degree of strengthening of the immune system must always be examined separately in *each* individual patient with *each* individual supplement. In general, if something makes you feel worse, don't take it. "No pain, no gain" is NOT the way to strengthen your immune system. Adults can probably take colostrum indefinitely, but babies, children, and teens should probably take it only when the immune system needs some acute boosting to fight an acute illness. More might be better for the young ones, but the long-term effects of the multiple growth factors present in colostrum need more study.

MSM

Methyl-sulfonyl-methane (MSM) also appears to be a supplement that usually results in positive clinical changes, even in patients who tend to detoxify too rapidly. MSM is a natural form of organic sulfur that is present in low concentrations throughout our tissues and body fluids. Many fresh foods, including fruits, vegetables, meat, and eggs, contain MSM. However, aging, processing, and cooking rapidly deplete the content of MSM in food. MSM is important in the ongoing synthesis of new proteins to help maintain healthy cells. Clinically, MSM appears to be another supplement that is supportive to good immune function.

ALOE VERA

Supplementation with products containing aloe vera can also work to support immune function. A carbohydrate fraction of the aloe vera plant called acemannan is considered by many to be the major active ingredient causing the predominant clinical effects. Acemannan has been shown to affect different aspects of the immune system in a positive fashion.[17–19] Monocytes, macrophages, and lymphocytes, important players in the immune response, have all been shown to respond positively to acemannan. When supplementing with aloe vera, be sure that the product is fresh, and that it contains significant amounts of acemannan.

COENZYME Q10

Another good supplement to consider taking regularly is coenzyme Q10 (CoQ10). CoQ10 is known to be crucial to the production of energy in all human cells. Langsjoen et al. demonstrated that patients with cardiomyopathy (poorly contracting heart muscle) who take CoQ10 have increased survival rates and increased strength of heart contraction.[20] CoQ10 has also been shown to be effective in helping to control the progress of breast cancer. Lockwood et al. demonstrated that taking this supplement can result in objective regression of breast tumors as well as regression of cancer at sites where it had spread beyond the breast.[21] Anything that can retard tumor growth is by definition strengthening the immune system. In fact, Folkers et al. demonstrated that taking CoQ10 reliably increased levels of immune globulins and protective lymphocytes.[22]

DHEA

Dehydroepiandrosterone (DHEA) is an important hormone produced by the adrenal gland in humans. Even though it is important as a building block for other important hormones, including estrogen and testosterone, its presence in the blood and throughout the body declines progressively with age. It is likely that many of the toxins faced on a daily basis help to accelerate this decline. The closer the levels of DHEA and the hormones produced from DHEA are to normal, the better immune function is supported.

Angele et al. recently demonstrated that DHEA acutely supported immune function in mice, so that survival following trauma was significantly improved.[23] Interestingly, even though DHEA can lead to increases in testosterone or estrogen, testosterone administration alone in the male mice actually depressed immune function after trauma. It appears that DHEA, as a precursor compound, tends to convert to the hormone that the body needs most to support immune function.

DHEA should probably always be supplemented when its blood levels, which can be measured, are low. Empirical trials of it can also be given to see if clinical benefit occurs when DHEA levels are only in the "low normal" range.

MONITORING SUPPLEMENTATION

Even when intelligently chosen, a given regimen of supplementation should not be undertaken and continued for life without any change, unless that regimen consistently results in a good clinical status and normal follow-up laboratory blood and hair testing. Be sure to work with a health care practitioner who will follow you closely and properly interpret your test results.

The primary rule of supplementation is never to ignore the clinical picture. If chronic symptoms of illness are lessening or even disappearing, you are on the right track. I never try to convince anyone to alter their regimen if they are objectively better clinically and staying that way. However, I do make them aware that continuing the same regimen indefinitely may not always be the best choice, especially after significant nutrient depletions have been restored. Continuing large doses of supplements after depletions have been resolved can "flip-flop" the patient into a gradually worsening state of "oversupplementation" toxicity.

A further consideration is especially important when the patient is detoxifying rapidly, as often occurs after dental toxicity has been removed. Sometimes the very minerals that restore clinical health also increase the rate at which cells can release their stored toxins. Such a detoxification also involves retoxification, since all released toxins do not get completely excreted. Some of them are redeposited into new cells, producing a new toxic effect in those cells. This possibility should always be considered when there is a return of symptomatology in a patient who initially responded very well. Detoxification must always proceed at a relatively *slow, controlled* rate, so that any retoxification will be adequately neutralized by an immune system well supported with optimal nutrition and optimal supplementation, such as megadose vitamin C.

When you are feeling well on a regimen of vitamins, minerals, and other supplements, you still should consider having some methodical follow-up by a well-qualified health care practitioner, utilizing routine blood, hair, and urine testing. Generally, if things are getting gradually out of balance, such testing can warn you before any clinical decline takes place. Clinical decline does not usually take place overnight, and a thorough review of regularly obtained tests will usually reveal a gradual deterioration of blood, hair, and urine chemistries before new symptoms develop or old symptoms recur. Practice preventive medicine. Having regular follow-ups is one of the best ways to maintain your good health. Many people are frightened at how quickly a friend or family member can be "struck down" while in seemingly good health. This type of follow-up could prevent many of these tragedies, since telltale signs usually appear well before this sudden loss of health.

As a *general* rule, blood chemistries for adults should be within the ranges listed in table 1. Dr. Huggins and I developed these ranges over time, as patients who underwent Total Dental Revision and followed good diets were retested. These were also the ranges that emerged most commonly in the patients who showed clinical improvement in their various disease processes. The ranges in parentheses are those commonly seen in most hospital laboratories and claimed to be the real approximate normal ranges of those laboratory tests in man. These ranges are much wider than the recommended ranges that are not enclosed by parentheses. This extra width allows for most of the population to register as normal. However, since most of the population is dealing with a lot of toxicity, their blood work does not contract into the narrower, healthier ranges until that toxicity has been neutralized or properly eliminated. Neither the public nor the medical profession would settle for a range of normalcy that excluded a majority of patients.

Table 1.		
OPTIMAL BLOOD CHEMISTRY RANGES		
Laboratory Test	Optimal Range	Usual Range
Calcium	9.4–9.7 mg/dL	(8.3–10.9)
Phosphorus	3.6–4.1 mg/dL	(2.5–4.9)
Glucose	75–85 mg/dL	(65–110)
Cholesterol	160–240 mg/dL	(125–275)
Triglycerides	<100 mg/dL	(20–200)
Uric acid	<5.0 mg/dL	(4.5–8.0)
Total protein	6.6–7.4 g/dL	(6.4–8.3)
Albumin	4.4–4.8 g/dL	(3.5–5.0)
Globulin	2.2–2.6 g/dL	(2.9–3.3)
BUN	13–17 mg/dL	(7–22)
Total bilirubin	<1.0 mg/dL	(0.2–1.5)
SGOT	<25 U/L	(10–42)
Hemoglobin	13–16 g/dL	(11.7–17.7)
Platelets	225–250 x 10^3/uL	(150–400)
White blood cells	5,000–6,000/uL	(3,500–11,000)
Lymphocytes	2,100–2,400/uL	(1,000–2,400)

If you compare these blood chemistry ranges with your own results, you may find that many or even most of your results fall within the ranges given in parentheses, but not within the more restrictive ranges before them. In fact, the huge assault of toxicity, led by the dental toxins that most people face, will keep these tests out of the narrower, optimal ranges.

A laboratory result of special concern is a low lymphocyte count. Generally speaking, the lower this count is, the less fighting power remains in the immune system. Dr. Huggins and I found that the sickest and most toxic patients consistently had the lowest lymphocyte counts. And when this level dipped below 1,000, it became less and less likely that the patient's immune system and the lymphocyte count would completely rebound even with the removal of dental toxicity and the support of optimal nutrition.

This observation recently received inadvertent support in the scientific literature. Ommen et al. found that the long-term survival of patients with congestive heart failure was significantly and independently related to lymphocyte count.[24] Although these researchers were looking only at the survival of heart failure patients, it is not hard to appreciate that the survival of any chronically diseased population would directly correlate with a test that indicates general immune system compromise from toxicity, such as low lymphocyte count.

It should also be noted that the natural response of white blood cells is to *increase* in the face of toxicity. A low white blood cell count, combined with a low lymphocyte count, is generally correlated with a long-term immune system exposure to toxicity, with the low cell counts representing somewhat of a "burned out" immune response to the unrelenting toxicity.

When toxins are properly removed and eliminated, the narrower laboratory ranges in the preceding chart are the ranges that are consistently seen to gradually appear. Many of your tests may never get in these tighter ranges, but these ranges should still be your targets, and you should attempt to get your chemistries to move toward this level of normalcy rather than away from it. These tests are especially important for the monitoring of proper detoxification after significant toxins such as dental toxins have been removed or minimized, since the detoxification process can get you just as sick as the primary exposure. The blood chemistries can rapidly deteriorate to where they were before toxins were ever removed if the rapid detoxification rate goes unchecked and unrecognized. Furthermore, this can occur even after years of good health if an ill-advised change in nutrition and supplementation again "kicks up" an excessive detoxification rate. Following these laboratory test results closely can prevent days, weeks, and even months of illness that will occur when they finally deteriorate to the point when immune compromise and clinical illness results.

The hair analysis is also very useful, although it is a little understood test. The levels of the elements that are reported on such a test reflect ONLY what was circulating in the blood while those hairs tested were actually growing. If you have large body stores of a toxic element, but your new exposure was minimal during the months when the tested hair was growing, your test result could be normal or even LOW. Conversely, if you had a recent high acute exposure to a toxic element, but your total body stores were low, the hair level could be very high.

Hair analysis is most useful in guiding supplementation and monitoring body levels of toxins when multiple tests taken over the course of many months or years are viewed together. Levels can shoot up and later drop down, usually indicating the bodily stores have been mobilized and excreted. High levels can drop down and then come back up to lower baseline levels, usually indicating that a storage of a nonbioavailable form of a mineral element, such as calcium or magnesium, has been excreted, allowing the reaccumulation of bioavailable forms. It's not too useful to run sequential hair analysis tests less than four to six months apart, since the changes that these tests measure move slowly. Blood testing is always more immediately useful, but the addition of hair analysis can help you to fine-tune your supplementation over the long term.

Urine testing for a heavy metal such as mercury can also serve to indicate how fast detoxification is proceeding. Since this detoxification rate is generally very critical to how healthy one is at the moment, such a test can be very useful as well. When a baseline urinary mercury level suddenly doubles or triples, increased exposure to mercury must be presumed, and this must come either from new outside sources or from within, due to an increased rate of detoxification. Furthermore, if the higher urine mercury level is indicating an increased rate of detoxification, it is not usually important to check other urinary heavy metals, since the levels of mercury in the urine will generally track the release rates of other heavy metals and toxins from their internal storage sites.

CONCLUSION

Much of the above detail might be confusing or just too much detail for some. However, it is important to realize that the pursuit of good health through proper supplementation is just not as straightforward or simple as we might like it to be. Furthermore, it should be apparent that improper supplementation is not only of little or no benefit, it can be an additional source of toxicity, either through overaccumulation of supplements or by overstimulation of detoxification. If this information overwhelms you or leaves you frustrated in your pursuit of good health, seek out a health care practitioner who appears to understand the principles presented and will help you incorporate them into your lifestyle. If you choose not to do this, then at least follow the principles that make good sense to you. Some improvement in your habits of supplementation is better than leaving the entire matter unaddressed.

TOXIC BLOCKS TO GOOD HEALTH AND OPTIMAL WEIGHT

OVERVIEW

Although much of what I'll say in this chapter may seem to be little more than common sense, the concepts to be presented are nevertheless not commonly recognized. Toxins play very prominent roles in blocking optimal nutrition, good health, and the achievement of ideal weight. At a very superficial level, it is only logical that any poison in the body will compromise the goals of good health and proper weight. However, some of the mechanisms by which toxins impair good health can be very indirect and inapparent. The better you understand how your body works and what can hurt you, the better you will be able to control your present and future state of health.

Toxicity, regardless of its source, can operate by one of at least two major mechanisms. Most toxins can exert a damaging effect by directly binding to various tissues and enzyme systems throughout the body. These tissues and enzymes will then be less capable of performing their normal function. And as these normal functions are impaired, abnormal compensatory functions can appear or even predominate. Toxins can also interfere with the ability of the immune system to properly protect your health. The immune system is complex, and the potential interactions of toxins with different immune system cells and other components are numerous. It is commonly accepted that a strong and competent immune system is the body's most important protection against disease. Any compromise of the immune system through toxicity is an important factor in compromising your good health.

DENTAL TOXICITY

At first blush, discussing the negatives of some dental fillings and other dental work might seem completely unrelated to achieving good nutrition, optimal health, and normal body size. However, the toxins in the typical mouth will often prevent the realization of these goals. In fact, dental toxins represent the largest amount of daily toxin exposure that most people experience—head and shoulders above pesticides, air pollution, fluoride, and other sources of environmental toxicity. You should avoid ALL toxin sources that are within your ability to control. Dental toxins are simply often the most significant toxins, and most people have the ability to control how much or how little toxicity they have in their mouths, once they have been completely informed. Aside from the expense and discomfort of visiting your dentist, being properly informed is the only real barrier between you and a toxin-free mouth.

MERCURY AND OTHER TOXIC METALS

For over a hundred years amalgam fillings have been the most commonly placed dental fillings. Amalgam fillings, known to much of the public as silver fillings, contain approximately 50 percent elemental mercury when they are initially placed. As I noted in chapter 2, mercury is the most toxic of the nonradioactive heavy metals. When a small amount of mercury is spilled today from a broken thermometer at an elementary school, the school is immediately closed for several days while hazardous material experts clean the area. Unfortunately, no one seems to treat the mouths of millions of people with the same regard as they show to the floor on which that drop of mercury fell.

Both in the finished amalgam and in its uncombined elemental state, mercury will continually produce mercury vapor. In the mouth, this vapor can be directly inhaled. Eggleston and Nylander found that vapor from only five amalgam fillings could increase brain mercury levels threefold over controls.[1] This mercury vapor can also be quickly converted to organic forms or inorganic salts in the mouth. And since swallowing is as continual an activity as breathing, the gastrointestinal tract gets a continual exposure to a variety of different mercury compounds.

As I also mentioned earlier, this ongoing assault from dental mercury promotes a wide variety of gut disorders. This means that the toxins originating in the mouth can harm the body not only by the direct toxic tissue effects and the toxic effects on the immune system mentioned earlier in this chapter, they also often have dramatic effects on the ability to properly digest. When you don't properly digest your food, you have even fewer good building blocks available to properly construct new proteins that neutralize toxicity. Furthermore, you end up producing even more toxins directly from the gut due to the poorly digested food and the proliferation of anaerobic bacteria and their exceptionally potent toxins. Mercury and the other dental toxins can effectively multiply their own more direct toxic effects to a substantial degree by their interference with proper digestive activity.

Aside from having a toxic effect on the gut, mercury is notorious for producing a wide variety of symptoms, some quite subtle. You may not be the hypochondriac that your doctors think you are.

Low-dose chronic mercury poisoning (micromercurialism), which can be caused by a mouthful of amalgams, can cause irritability, depression, insomnia, nervousness, mild tremor, impaired judgment and coordination, decreased ability to think clearly, emotional instability, headache, fatigue, and loss of sex drive. And any of these symptoms, once initiated by mercury toxicity, can become profoundly worse when the immune system is further stressed by any additional sources of toxicity. These symptoms are so common that many people accept them as part of life, or as just part of growing older. This is not surprising, since nearly the entire population of the United States has amalgam fillings.

Although mercury is the predominant toxin in the amalgam filling, it should also be remembered that these fillings will usually also contain variable amounts of silver, copper, tin, and zinc. Many metals that are of benefit to the body in the form of an organic or inorganic salt can be highly toxic in their chemically unbound and elemental forms. Copper would be an especially good example of this. Among other effects, copper excess can promote a pro-oxidant state in the body which produces excessive amounts of free radicals.

Amalgams are relatively inexpensive fillings, and their mechanical properties make them durable and relatively easy to place for the dentist. Unfortunately, the field of dentistry has rarely ever concerned itself with the toxicologic study of the materials it uses and promotes. As long as the mechanical properties of a filling are desirable, little or no thought is given or has ever been given to the toxic effects of any of the filling components.

Nickel is another metal commonly used in dentistry that is highly toxic. Nickel has already been identified as a cancer-causing agent. Sunderman published a review on the many different ways in which nickel can induce cancer.[2] Of significant interest, then, is that stainless steel is typically a nickel alloy. This means that the multiple usages of stainless steel in the mouth can result in a chronic nickel exposure. Partial dentures often contain some stainless steel.

Crowns, or caps, often contain nickel in the bases that adhere to the tooth stumps. The stainless steel braces that have been placed in the mouths of so many of our youngsters can also be expected to offer a chronic nickel exposure. Any cursory review of nickel on MED-LINE will reveal numerous studies on the various toxic effects and cancer-causing properties of nickel. Yet most dentists and medical doctors still seem unconcerned about permanently inserting this metal inside the human body. One may well wonder if any study could be dramatic enough to make this practice stop. Do you really want your child to have nickel braces inside the mouth for several years? Unless you protest to your orthodontist, that is exactly what will happen, at least for the time being.

Certain chemicals in some replacement fillings can be just as bad for your health as amalgam fillings. Composite, nonmetal fillings are numerous in number and very diverse in content. At least up until now, modern dental technology has focused almost exclusively on the final physical and mechanical properties of the composite filling. It seems as if the toxic properties of the individual chemicals in a dental product are deemed irrelevant as long as the final product is easy to handle and install. When getting amalgams and other fillings replaced, consider using a specialized blood test to see which filling materials are least reactive with your immune system (see Appendix II).

DENTAL INFECTIONS

Incredibly, mercury is not the worst toxin in many people's mouths. In fact, mercury will nearly always take second place when one or more root canal–treated teeth are in the mouth. With very rare exception, the technique used in performing a root canal will introduce bacteria from the mouth deep into the root of the tooth or allow bacteria already present to escape elimination by the immune system. This means that bacteria that operate normally in the oxygen-containing environment of the mouth are subjected to the oxygen-starved environment of the tooth root tip and the internal tooth pulp. When these oxygen-requiring bacteria are deprived of their oxygen, their metabolism undergoes a radical transformation. Enormously toxic by-products begin to be produced under these circumstances. The waste products of this oxygen-deprived metabolism are enormously toxic. In fact, they have been demonstrated in unpublished tests to have toxic effects on some human enzymes that are many times greater than the toxic effects of *Clostridium botulinum.* When one realizes that traditional scientists and doctors still consider botulinum toxin to be the most potent toxin known, the implications of this anaerobic oral toxicity are enormous. Viewed from a different perspective, a root canal tooth could be considered a little manufacturing plant for the low-grade and chronic production of toxins substantially more toxic than botulinum toxin. Death from a root canal rarely occurs quickly since this chronic release of the toxins is very small in amount, although it is continuous. However, there could hardly exist a better and more subtle way to chronically traumatize the immune system. The immune system will generally compensate for toxicity as long as it can, and then collapse rather suddenly months or even years after the root canal. Relatively good health can be maintained until this collapse, and the correlation between the infected root canal tooth and the heart attack, cancer, or other degenerative disease is rarely made.

Another very significant source of dental infective toxicity comes from periodontal disease, or disease of the gums. Chronic gum disease can harbor the same types of bacteria that are seen with root canals, and the same types of extremely potent anaerobic bacterial toxins can result. Scannapieco and Genco outlined the evidence supporting the association between periodontal disease and both heart and lung disease.[3] Beck et al. also demonstrated that periodontal disease is probably a significant risk factor for both heart attack and stroke.[4] Interestingly, smoking, which has long been recognized as a risk factor for heart attack, is also the single best way to assure the eventual development of periodontal disease. Perhaps one of the main ways that smoking causes heart disease is by causing periodontal disease with all of its infective toxicity. Aside from avoiding smoking and taking large doses of vitamin C, the regular use of a dental water irrigation device with some hydrogen peroxide added to the irrigating water is one of the best ways to maintain healthy gums.

CAVITATIONS

Another little known but highly toxic dental condition is the cavitation. When the larger teeth are removed in the standard dental fashion, cavitations will commonly result.[5] The tooth sits in a shock-absorbing hammock called the periodontal ligament. This ligament separates the tooth from the surrounding jawbone. When this ligament is not also removed with the tooth, incomplete healing of the remaining hole can be anticipated. Generally, the ligament will not attach strongly enough to the tooth to be removed as well, and a brief but additional procedure is necessary to remove it after the tooth has been extracted. When the ligament is allowed to remain, the surrounding jawbone has no "realization" that the tooth inside the ligament is gone, and there is no natural signal for bone growth to commence across the ligament and into the hole. Instead, bone heals over the top of the hole from the upper edges of the extraction site, where there is no ligament separating the bone cells from the hole. Since the bacteria of the mouth will always get into this hole before the cap heals over, toxins will develop and accumulate in this cavitation hole after the seal is complete and no oxygen is available, just as they do in the case of a root canal.

Pathologically, a cavitation represents a focus of wet gangrene in the jawbone. Any doctor will tell you that the only treatment for gangrene anywhere in the body is either amputation or a complete cleaning out of the area. Yet most people, thanks to the almost routine extraction of wisdom teeth, have several of these gangrenous pockets in their jawbones. Typically these cavitations remain unaddressed for life, yet they are a source of continuous and chronic poisoning.

Without even realizing the existence of cavitations as a routine occurrence following dental extractions, Joshipura et al. published a study showing that tooth loss is also associated with cardiovascular disease.[6] It would seem that these cavitations represent one more independent risk factor for heart disease, and, undoubtedly, all the other diseases that are aggravated by unneutralized toxicity.

Dental Implants

A typical dental implant is inserted at a prior extraction site before the bone has completely healed. Since most routine extractions are actually cavitations in the process of forming, an implant is often being inserted through a pocket of developing gangrene. When a metallic screw, especially one made of the nickel-containing stainless steel, is implanted into the jawbone through this forming cavitation, metallic toxicity and anaerobic bacterial toxicity are almost certain to be introduced deep into the jawbone. Since this is the typical way in which implants are done, it is still not really known if the implant could be an immunologically acceptable restoration if uninfected healing could be documented after a proper extraction and before the implant, while using an implant metal of only minimal toxicity.

A word about dentures. Since most extractions routinely leave in the periodontal ligaments, most people who have had all of their teeth removed have a huge number of cavitations, often connecting together in a tubelike fashion over much of the jawbone. This can be highly toxic. The sickest people who came to Dr. Huggins's clinic to have their dental toxins removed usually had the fewest teeth, and had one or more root canals in the few teeth that remained.

GETTING RID OF DENTAL TOXINS

Getting rid of dental toxins is not as simple and straightforward as one might hope. Blood testing to determine what replacement materials are least burdensome to your immune system is available, although not widely. Detoxification after such dental work is also a complex process. When most of the dental toxicity is removed, the spontaneous detoxification of the rest of the body is typically very brisk, needing no detoxification accelerators. Done completely wrong without proper attention to detail, the removal of dental toxins can aggravate your medical conditions. The removal process and the subsequent detoxification process can both be done in either a highly toxic fashion or a safe and only minimally toxic fashion. Thus, it is essential to find a dentist who is well educated on these matters. The last thing you need is a dentist who is just humoring your "eccentricities" and not paying close attention to the above details. For further help in these matters, see Appendix II at the end of the book.

CUMULATIVE IMMUNE SYSTEM SUPPRESSION

Although the concept of cumulative toxicity on immune system function has already been addressed, it must also be emphasized that the immune system will often only demonstrate the effects of the cumulative toxicity in a sudden, dramatic fashion clinically. Furthermore, the many different insults that finally caused the immune system to "collapse" may have been present for months, years, or even decades prior to the loss of health. This is probably the primary reason why long-term toxin exposure still gets so little blame for the devastating damage that it causes. Other biological systems will typically demonstrate a gradual erosion of function over time. Not the immune system, however. Even if certain aspects of the immune system do gradually become compromised from prolonged toxic exposure, the intact organism, in this case the human, will usually compensate in a variety of different ways. This gives the distinct impression that good health is very suddenly and dramatically replaced with a new disease process. The patient literally seems to "fall off the cliff" rather than to gradually stumble down the hill.

Coogan et al. published a study showing that men who survive cancer in one testicle are at much greater risk of developing cancer in the other testicle, sometimes as long as twenty-five years later.[7] One way to look at this information is to realize that whatever compromised the immune system enough to allow the first cancer to appear can smolder in the background for over two decades until the second cancer appears. Toxicity, especially chronic and low-grade toxicity, could be expected to manifest itself in exactly this fashion. Almost by definition, anyone who has ever had cancer has a severely compromised immune system and any unaddressed toxicity will increase the likelihood that a new cancer or other degenerative disease process will appear later. When a cancer goes into remission or is clinically cured, but toxic exposures continue, the patient is really just a clinical time bomb waiting for an opportunity to explode.

ELECTROMAGNETIC TOXICITY

Toxicity is not always something that has a tangible, physically substantive nature. Anything that will prove to be an additional stress to the immune system can be considered a toxin. Most of the electromagnetic, radio wave, and microwave fields that we are immersed in on a daily basis are inescapable. However, as with toxins of any source, being subjected unwittingly to inescapable toxicity is not a good reason for making no effort to avoid completely *escapable* toxicity. Any immune system stresses that you can avoid or remove will make it that much easier (or less difficult) to maintain your health in the face of the toxicity that you cannot remove or avoid.

Much of the dental work performed years ago at the clinic of Dr. Hal Huggins was performed in a dental operatory surrounded by a Faraday cage. A Faraday cage is an enclosure designed to keep any ambient electric charge sitting on its outer, conductive surface. This design prevents an electrostatic field from being present within the area surrounded by the conductive surface. This unique phenomenon, known as the Faraday cage effect, is traditionally utilized to shield electronic equipment from unwanted electrostatic fields present in the immediate environment.

The human body also has its own very delicate electrical and electromagnetic fields. A Faraday cage was added to the dental operatory in the hope that it would filter out some of the many sources of electromagnetic waves surrounding us constantly. Empirically, the sicker patients seemed to recover more readily when their dental work was performed in this special operatory. Seizure patients especially seemed to respond better in this environment. Certainly, the natural human electromagnetic forces are of a very tiny magnitude relative to the other known man-made or natural sources of such forces, and it should come as no surprise that this subtle human electromagnetism can be disrupted, altered, and/or inhibited fairly easily. Perhaps as more people become aware of the negative effects that these many sources of radiation have on their health, houses, bedrooms, places of work, and other areas where they spend much of their time, increasing efforts will be made to provide protection from the cumulative exposure to these radiant energy sources, further protecting our increasingly compromised immune systems.

Patients who came to the clinic of Dr. Huggins also routinely received chiropractic evaluation and manipulation. Most of the patients received an objective evaluation of muscular tenderness before and after the two-week treatment protocol, measuring the pain response to a device that transmitted a measurable amount of pressure to different sites of the body. Typically, at the end of the clinic visit, muscles and muscular attachment sites in the neck, shoulders, lower back, and buttocks would demonstrate two- or even threefold less pain sensitivity to pressure than when first measured. The evaluation was made in a blinded fashion, such that old readings were not known to the measurer prior to making the new readings.

These pain threshold measurements were a useful tool in evaluating the effectiveness of chiropractic adjustment, as well as in making an initial assessment of the results of the Total Dental Revision protocol (which included proper nutrition and supplementation, as I explained earlier). It was not uncommon to see immediate positive changes in these pain thresholds directly following neck and back adjustments.

Somewhere along the way, another incredible observation was made. Patients were sometimes asked to remove their watches and other jewelry in the course of getting a chiropractic adjustment. It was immediately noted that in nearly every patient, all of the pain thresholds measured would be lower when a watch was worn and higher when the watch was taken off. Furthermore, in greater than 90 percent of all patients tested, the wearing of a battery-powered watch would result in the *physical shortening* of one leg relative to the other, reversible within seconds after the watch was removed. One leg was often an inch or more shorter than the other, not a subtle change open to interpretive argument. And it didn't matter where the watch was placed, held, or worn on the body. Tiny batteries that were considered spent were also tested against the body, and the same effect was seen. It didn't seem that a battery could be dead enough not to dramatically affect the body and its delicate electromagnetic circuitry.

Generally, plain metal did not have this effect, but it should also be noted that one wheelchair-bound patient with the immune system compromise seen with advanced multiple sclerosis actually showed the same effect of objective leg shortening from his Rolex watch, which did not contain a battery but did contain a large amount of metal. Once again, these findings should alert all clinicians, as well as patients, that the body is exquisitely sensitive to many influences that are not readily detected by our five senses. It should also heighten the awareness of potential toxicity from the ubiquitous pagers, cellular phones, and many other battery-powered devices that we keep so close to our bodies for so much of the day. The findings that were repeatedly seen when batteries or battery-containing devices neared the body are a strong indicator that using such modalities as the Faraday cage to screen out unwanted electromagnetic waves might not be so crazy after all.

The ultimate goal being promoted here is simple, even if it is difficult to accomplish: Give the body pure food, air, and water, and avoid all possible toxicity contamination, including that which cannot be tasted, smelled, felt, seen, or heard.

MAGNETIC THERAPIES

Further evidence of the subtle electromagnetic forces throughout the human body is seen when one looks at what happens when static magnetic fields are applied to the body or other biological systems. Trappier et al. published a study that looked at the effects of magnetic fields on human lung carcinoma (cancer) cells.[8] When the cancer cells were exposed to the negative polarity of the north pole of a 3.5 kilogauss magnet, growth dramatically slowed, almost stopping completely after five days of exposure! Conversely, the positive polarity of the south pole of the same magnet measurably *accelerated* the growth rate of the same cancer cells when exposed for a comparable period of time. The conclusion to be taken from this is that magnetic fields have definite effects on biological systems, and that the opposite poles of a static magnet can have opposite physiological effects.

Magnetic therapy is currently undergoing a wave of acceptance across the world, but many companies that produce magnets do not differentiate between the poles in their products. Avoid long-term exposure to the positive pole (south pole) of a magnet. The positive pole can encourage cancer growth, promote infection, and increase inflammation and pain. But the negative pole of a magnet can be a tremendous therapeutic tool, and it can exert supportive and strengthening effects on the immune system. If you are interested in biomagnetic therapies and are seeking a trustworthy source of information, check the resources listed in Appendix II. Finally, Davis and Rawls wrote a series of short books in the 1970s that details the tremendous potential of properly applied magnetic fields.[9–12]

PRACTICAL SUGGESTIONS

So far, I have told you mostly what you shouldn't do or eat and why you shouldn't do it or eat it. For any complete nutrition program to work, most people need some sort of formula outlining what they *should* do and what they *should* eat. In this chapter, I will outline the best ways to choose foods, combine those foods, and select and dose supplements. Although no one program of nutrition and supplementation will be best for everyone, most readers should be able to modify my basic program to fit their own individual health needs.

With rare exceptions, the recommendations that follow apply in general to everybody. Most of the diets that put different people in different dietary categories, such as the diet based on a person's blood type, do not recognize the very important contributions of food combination and toxin exposure reduction to the proper digestion and assimilation of food. When such factors are ignored or just not appreciated, individual sensitivities to different kinds of food will become much more pronounced.

It is true that some people are enzymatically and constitutionally much better equipped to properly digest some foods than others. However, everybody needs the proper balance and amounts of cholesterol, fats, and protein in their diet, or health will eventually become compromised as increasing toxin challenges are not met and defeated. Certainly, if one specific food consistently disagrees with you no matter how you eat or combine it, you should avoid it. But do not assume that one poorly digested food out of a group bars the whole group. You should not give up all meat because beef does not agree with you anymore than you should give up all vegetables because carrots do not agree with you. Poorly tolerated beef should not eliminate turkey, chicken, and lamb from your diet as well.

FACTORS THAT SUPPORT GOOD DIGESTION

The following factors have already been addressed earlier in some detail. Each one is critical in the proper digestion of high-quality food. The benefit of one factor may not be as apparent in one person as it is in another person. The goal is to incorporate all of these factors into a regular program of nutrition.

FACTORS THAT SUPPORT GOOD NUTRITION

1. *Chew.* All your food should have a smooth texture, free of lumpiness, before you swallow it.
2. *Don't drink liquids while eating.* Drinking with a meal should be minimized, and even eliminated if possible. Drink no more than 1 cup of liquid, room temperature or warmer, and neither acidic nor alkaline (such as water). The liquid in a soup is of course okay and is not considered something to be avoided.
3. *Take good supplemental enzymes.* Take them fifteen to thirty minutes before a meal. Generally, supplemental enzymes will be most useful before a meal that contains significant amounts of protein.
4. *Don't drink alcohol.* If you do not want to give up alcohol completely, at least do not use it as a beverage with your meal.

5. *Eat small meals frequently.* Even if you require more food than most people need for sustenance, eating most or all of it in one sitting will result in vastly poorer digestion and nutrition than eating the same amount of food in several sittings.
6. *Develop a routine.* Your digestive system will be most efficient if you consistently eat at the same times every day. However, don't feel compelled to eat if you are not hungry.
7. *Avoid stress with your meal.* Acute stress is a strong impediment to good digestion. It would be better just to have a light snack at mealtime, and then eat the substantive meal when you are feeling less stressed. Conversely, if stress gives you an appetite, try to find ways other than eating to cope with that stress.

PROPER FOOD COMBINING

Go by the "numbers":
1. Starches and complex carbohydrates (not simple sugars)
2. Fats and vegetables (except for vegetables that are high in starch)
3. Protein (other than vegetable protein)
4. Fruit
5. Dairy products

Suggested combinations:
-   Eat 1 with 2.
-   Eat 2 with 3.
-   Never eat 1 with 3.
-   Eat 4 by itself, and never sooner than two to four hours after a meal.
-   Eat 5 by itself, and never sooner than two to four hours after a meal.

Remember that it can sometimes be difficult to avoid improper food combinations completely. Whenever possible, minimize the impact of a bad combination. If you are at a dinner party where your hostess has labored long and hard, have no more than half of a very small baked potato to go with your meat. If possible, replace the potato or a portion of the potato with a larger portion of whatever nonstarchy vegetable is being offered. When you cannot avoid a poor combination, chewing thoroughly, drinking little or no liquid, and following the other suggestions that support good nutrition assume even greater importance. Take advantage of as many of these factors as you can in a given situation.

THREE-DAY MENU WITH PROPER FOOD COMBINING PRINCIPLES

When considering how you want to eat, you must first determine whether you want to lose weight. If so, you must identify and minimize the eating of foods with glycemic index scores greater than about 60 (see Appendix I). Regardless of the glycemic index of the foods you eat, they should always be eaten in a properly combined fashion to optimize their benefits to your health. Proper food combining will also help you to achieve and maintain optimal weight.

Day One
Breakfast:

Start the day with a quart of purified water upon awakening. Then have whatever raw fruits you enjoy, in any combination. If you're still hungry, wait thirty minutes and have

- One or two eggs, cooked any way you like. If you fry them, use butter.
- One or two corn tortillas as a bread substitute.
- Portion of sautéed ham, sausage, or steak.
- Decaffeinated coffee or tea.

Lunch:

It's better to eat most of the day's calories at midday than in the evening. Have

- Salad with lettuce and choice of vegetables (tomato, carrot, celery, heart of palm, fresh beets, etc.). For dressings, choose fresh lemon juice or an oil-based dressing. Creamy dressings are acceptable if made with cream rather than milk. If you choose a dressing that doesn't appear to be a good combination, use only 1 to 2 teaspoons.
- Grilled hamburger steak with sautéed onions.

Dinner:

Eat light at night. Consider having just a medley of vegetables occasionally, even if you are a dedicated eater of meat, or at least limit the amount of meat you eat at night to 1 or 2 ounces.

- Use a wok to make a quick sautéed combination of green peppers, broccoli, onion, corn, sprouts, and fresh tomato. If desired, add a small amount of cubed chicken or beef. Have this alone or with a small garden salad.

Day Two
Breakfast:

Continue as with Day One, drinking a quart of purified water upon awakening. If you're not in the mood for fruit, go straight to a more traditional breakfast.

- Cooked oatmeal topped with a nondairy milk like Rice Dream, or with table cream diluted with water or nut milk, at a ratio of 1 to 3.
- Toast and butter.
- Decaffeinated coffee or tea.

Lunch:

- Vegetable soup (traditional or creamed).
- Grilled chicken breast.

Dinner:

- Freshly steamed rice with butter and choice of legume, including black-eyed peas, kidney beans, or lima beans.
- One sliced tomato, with or without dressing. The tomato may also be stuffed—with chicken salad, for example.

Day Three
Breakfast:

- One quart of water upon awakening.
- Two-egg omelet, with onions, cheese, and diced chicken or steak. Add sautéed green pepper or mushrooms, if desired.

Lunch:

- Steamed broccoli and cauliflower with butter.
- Beef and vegetable stew.

Dinner:

- Spelt pasta with butter and tomato sauce.
- Fresh garden salad.

These menus are only suggestions. They will give you an idea of how to enjoy eating with proper food combining. Remember that you should eat yogurt and other dairy products separately, several hours after a meal as a snack, or as an early morning snack in lieu of a more traditional breakfast. The exception is cheese, which can be combined with other proteins at mealtime. You can drink fruit juice at any time before a meal, as long as you drink it several hours after the last meal. Vegetable juices combine well and can be taken at any time.

CALORIC CONSUMPTION

In general, the above factors and food combination considerations will not only give you optimal nutrition, they will also facilitate normalization of body size. Overweight individuals will tend to lose weight, and excessively thin individuals will tend to gain weight. Furthermore, if these considerations are strictly heeded, weight loss can easily be accomplished without ever having to deal with the pangs of hunger. Certain food combinations can never be consumed, but hunger can usually be completely avoided.

For the overweight person who does not lose weight after closely following the above regimen, foods with a high glycemic index rating must be avoided as completely as possible. Chronically high insulin levels must eventually come down for the weight loss to result, and this simply will not happen with the regular consumption of such foods as white flour, white rice, potatoes, and corn. A table listing the glycemic indexes of common foods is included in Appendix I of this book. For one without a weight problem, high glycemic index foods can be consumed as long as the proper food combination principles are followed. However, whether you are overweight or not, the foods with the highest glycemic indexes should be minimized since they do metabolically stress the body from the wide and rapid fluctuations of glucose seen with their ingestion.

ADDITIONAL SUGGESTIONS

A number of individual items are presented here. Singly, many of them would have only a minor impact on the overall quality of one's nutrition. However, collectively, the impact on nutritional quality can be substantial. Remember, the more recommendations that are followed, the better. Failing to follow all recommendations does not mean you are destined to nutritive failure. Individual circumstances will always dictate varying degrees of compliance. If your present eating regimen is very far removed from these recommendations, try to gradually align yourself with this regimen. When changes are too drastic and too abrupt, we tend not to follow them. We are all creatures of habit, and gradualism is sometimes the best way to achieve permanent changes. When you see the positive effects that optimal nutrition has on your health and physical appearance, you will have all the motivation you need to continue this program for the rest of your life.

1. Do not avoid sources of good natural fat in your diet. Do avoid as much as possible the hydrogenated fats found in processed foods. Never eat foods that have been stripped of natural fat and are advertised as low fat or fat free.
2. Never eat margarine or other butter substitutes.
3. Eat butter regularly. Include it routinely with most meat and vegetable dishes, because it aids in the absorption and assimilation of the vitamins, minerals, and other nutrients in those foods.
4. Cook mostly with butter or olive oil.
5. Avoid or minimize your consumption of all processed and preserved foods. Exceptions would include properly dried foods without preservatives. Shop frequently and eat food that is as fresh as possible.
6. Avoid or minimize your consumption of pork and pork-related products (ham, bacon, sausage).
7. Avoid or minimize your consumption of fish and other seafood. Pregnant women should avoid seafood completely.
8. Whenever possible, eat organically raised foods.
9. Do not eat irradiated food. The nutrient value of food is lowered by irradiation, which can also form toxic

by-products inside the food. Also, irradiation kills bacteria but not poisons, so bad food that is already toxic will not rot, smell, and so warn you not to eat it.

10. Eat a variety of meats (but not in combination). If possible, eat some wild game.

11. Eat whole fruits and vegetables rather than juicing them. Juices that include the pulp are acceptable. However, juices are much more desirable than nearly all commercial drinks. Never routinely substitute juices for a full, balanced meal.

12. Use salt as desired for taste. Restrict its intake only if you are advised to do so by your physician. Always use the purest sodium chloride available. Avoid sea salt.

13. Eat grains that have been processed as little as possible. Organic grains are best, since they contain less fluoride and other contaminants from standard fertilizers, and contain more bioavailable vitamins and minerals.

14. Eat a variety of grains, but try to eat only one kind at a sitting. Good digestion is supported by simplicity in the meal, and multigrain products are not as readily and completely digested.

15. Avoid pasteurized animal milks with cereal. Nut milks are an excellent substitute; they combine well with grains and cereals, and unlike most dairy products, they are not toxic. If you cannot give up the taste of cow's milk, combine full organic cream with either water, Rice Dream, or a nut milk. A very small amount of cream diluted in this fashion gives a great taste, and by using so little cream, you avoid most of the problems associated with drinking milk, including its toxicity and its poor combining with the cereal grain.

16. Eat eggs regularly, but chew them completely, regardless of how they are cooked.

17. Avoid toxicity rather than cholesterol (see chapter 5).

18. Generally, try to cook foods at lower temperatures for longer periods of time. Whenever possible, cook by baking, broiling, poaching, or simmering in a crockpot. Minimize frying, although a quick sauté, as in a wok, is a reasonable compromise. Pressure cooking is a good way to minimize the loss of nutrients that occurs during cooking.

19. Eat raw foods often. Whenever possible, eat meats rare, not well done. Meat juices contain substantial amounts of bioavailable nutrients.

20. Avoid refined sugar as much as possible, and never consume it as a dessert following a regular meal. Eat sugar only well after a meal or at least an hour before the next meal.

21. If you are not allergic, sweeten your food sparingly with raw honey. The nutritional food supplement stevia can also be added to food or beverages for its nutrient and sweetening effects. Avoid aspartame and saccharin completely. Use other sweeteners as little as possible.

22. Drink distilled water or water purified by reverse osmosis. Try to drink at least 2 quarts of water a day. Drink at least 1 quart first thing upon arising, before eating breakfast or taking supplements. Space the rest of your water consumption out so as not to impair the digestion of foods that you eat during the day.

23. Avoid caffeine as completely as possible.

24. Minimize your consumption of regular and herbal teas, which may contain variable amounts of fluoride in addition to caffeine.

25. Avoid or minimize your consumption of carbonated sodas. When you do indulge, drink those sweetened with fruit juices or fructose.

26. Avoid or minimize your consumption of alcohol, especially with meals. Remember that beer contains maltose, which has about the highest glycemic index of any food substance. Avoid American wines in favor of German, French, or Italian wines. American wines contain an incredible number of additives and adulterants.

27. Avoid monosodium glutamate (MSG). It is toxic in itself, and it can mask the taste of partially spoiled food. When traveling by airplane, request a sodium-free meal (eliminating MSG), and then add sodium chloride as desired.

28. Wash all fruits and vegetables, scrubbing anything that can be scrubbed. Dilute hydrogen peroxide is one good cleanser. Fit, a commercially available preparation that contains citric acid, baking soda, and grapefruit seed oil, also works well. Be especially diligent in removing wax coatings.

29. Store food in glass rather than in plastic.

30. Use enameled iron or glass cookware, such as that made by Le Creuset and Pyrex. Avoid aluminum and stainless steel whenever possible.

31. Generally avoid mushrooms. If you eat them, cook them thoroughly.

32. Enjoy nuts and seeds, but chew them extremely thoroughly. Whenever possible, eat them raw.

33. Avoid foods that you consistently do not digest well. They will compromise the proper digestion of foods eaten with them.

34. Take only bioavailable vitamins and supplements (see chapter 8).

35. Take your optimal dose of vitamin C regularly. Consider doing frequent C-flushes to minimize the presence of toxic, rotting food in the intestines (see chapter 8).

This is by no means a complete or definitive list of guidelines. However, following all of these guidelines will help your body to ingest, absorb, assimilate, and eventually use all of the nutrients that you need to maintain optimal health. You may well discover many other ways to optimize your own nutrition as you become more attuned to your body and begin to learn what it appreciates having put into it.

MINIMIZE EXPOSURE TO TOXINS

While the proper diet, properly digested, is an enormously significant factor in maintaining or regaining good health, it will not be enough to help you if you are facing an enormous daily exposure to toxins. Dental toxicity must be addressed and eliminated as completely as possible before many people can begin to benefit from good nutrition. You simply cannot dry off while you are still in the shower. Good nutrition will always be a positive factor in seeking good health, but when daily toxin exposure goes above a certain level and stays there, good nutrition will not appear to be very effective in making you healthy. These issues are addressed in greater detail in *Uninformed Consent: The Hidden Dangers in Dental Care*[1], which I wrote in collaboration with Hal Huggins, and *It's All in Your Head: The Link Between Mercury Amalgams and Illness*, by Dr. Huggins.[2]

Toxins can also rear their ugly head when a well-motivated individual undergoes any of a number of different programs of detoxification, including some that are administered under the guidance of a doctor. Many such programs detoxify too rapidly, and even someone who is practicing the principles of optimal nutrition cannot maintain good health in the face of too-rapid detoxification. This issue is addressed in greater depth in *Uninformed Consent.*

A FINAL NOTE
FROM THE AUTHOR

In this book, a program of nutrition with an associated body of knowledge is presented that actually achieves the goal of good nutrition: a healthier body. Much of the information presented here was originally assembled from the groundbreaking work of Drs. Weston Price and Melvin Page, which I have described elsewhere in this book. Briefly, these two researchers found that certain foods clearly support good health and normal blood chemistries, while other foods do not. Overweight people lost weight and sick people felt better when they followed these nutritional recommendations.

As time went by, more and more of these recommendations were found to have solid support in scientific literature, as research cited throughout this book demonstrates. As more and more people follow the advice presented here, I hope to gain information that will enable me to refine that advice even further. However, no political agenda has motivated any recommendation made. Your feedback is welcome.

One of the more difficult recommendations I stress in this book is the necessity of meat in the diet. I respect all forms of life, and I certainly do not claim to understand all of the interrelationships among them. However, I know that most sick people will never realize their optimal physical health on a vegetarian diet. Perhaps remaining vegetarian while aware of that knowledge would make that individual an even more enlightened being. I cannot say at what point some principles become more important than life and health. That is an individual decision. However, as a physician who has worked in this area for a very long time, I feel that my primary obligation is to be true to the physiological facts of nutrition and minimize any of my personal thoughts as to any perceived moral rightness or wrongness of a way of eating and living. Although I personally eat meat regularly, since I promptly feel poorly completely off of it, I would not contest anybody's decision to abstain from meat. Everyone makes choices and has reasons for making those choices. Perhaps it is nothing more than a rationalization to believe that you can eat an animal and still respect it. I don't know. I just know that eating meat is the best way to keep your physical health intact and your body chemistries balanced.

As a physician and a scientist, there is little that bothers me more than having unsubstantiated opinions pass as facts. For this reason, I have tried wherever possible to demonstrate that most of the less conventional assertions in this book have support in the mainstream medical and scientific literature. The articles cited often focused on other points, while inadvertently supporting one or more of the assertions that I make in this book.

However, it is also important that all valid observations are not just thrown out as being "anecdotal" simply because they did not make their way to the promised land of published, peer-reviewed studies in the refereed scientific literature. Many established and respected journals routinely publish what are called "case reports." These case reports fatten up a university-based researcher's curriculum vitae just as effectively as more extensive studies requiring far more work and effort. However, a case report is little more than an anecdote. The only real difference between the two is the integrity and academic qualifications of the reporting observer. When the observer reports an observation of cause-and-effect in a single patient that supports the ongoing and accepted science of the moment, it is lauded and published as a case report. However, when it results in a conclusion that is contrary with any scientific lore of long standing, the information is attacked as anecdotal and the observer is vilified regardless of the quality of academic credentials possessed by that observer. Not surprisingly, such "anecdotes" are never given the opportunity to be formally published as case reports. The scientific lore of the moment possesses a very strong sense of self-preservation.

Why go into all of this detail on how scientific information is accepted, and, more commonly, rejected? Quite simply, because the more aware and educated you are as a consumer of scientific information and recommendations, the better off you will be. Scientists and physicians absolutely scorn anyone without formal training who would presume to question their conclusions or their methods of research. However, as we enter the next millennium, the Internet and the World Wide Web have changed all the rules. There is more information readily available on every subject imaginable than there ever has been before. While all of the information on the Internet is not correct, scientific controversies and differences of opinion can no longer be hidden so easily. MEDLINE research is readily accessible to anyone who wants to look. Phrases such as "Numerous studies show . . ." or "There is no credible scientific evidence to show that. . ." can easily be checked out. Exaggeration and misrepresentation of facts, data, and studies become readily apparent to those who want to look for themselves. The Internet has permanently pried open Pandora's box, and everybody in every field is accountable in a way that never existed before.

It is in this context that I have addressed the somewhat elusive and nebulous concept of optimal nutrition. For every statement made in this book, you can surely find plenty of "experts" who will tell you that the author is misguided at best, and at worst must have one or more hidden agendas to justify promulgating such amazing and obviously harmful statements about nutrition. However, you are now armed, aware, and—I hope—motivated. After all, it is your health and your life that are being affected. If I am wrong about anything of substance in this book, I welcome being told so, and I welcome being educated as to why I am wrong. Being wrong does not scare me, and it should not scare anyone else. It's high time that the quest for the truth and the pure desire to help others be the only reasons why people become doctors and scientists.

APPENDIX I

THE GLYCEMIC INDEX

The glycemic index (see also chapter 3) is a practical, scientific way of comparing the rate at which different foods release glucose into the blood. Food with carbohydrate content that breaks down rapidly and spikes glucose quickly into the blood will have a high glycemic index. Food with carbohydrate content that breaks down less rapidly and releases glucose into the blood more gradually will have a lower glycemic index. All of the numbers are relative to the rate at which glucose itself is absorbed into the blood. Some tables will assign glucose a value of 100 for comparison. In this table, under the testing methodology used, the average value for glucose was determined to be 97.

The following table provides a very general guide to the glycemic indexes of some common foods. More detailed information can be obtained from the sources from which these data were compiled.

GLYCEMIC INDEX COMPOSITE TABLE

Food Tested	Glycemic Index Mean (Glucose = 100)
Bakery Goods	
Cake	
Angel food	67
Banana, no sugar	55
Pound	54
Sponge	46
Croissant	67
Doughnut, cake-type	76
Muffins (eight studies)	62
Waffles (Aunt Jemima)	76
Breads	
Bagel, white	72
Banana bread	47
Barley kernel	
(75–80% kernels, three studies)	34
Barley flour (two studies)	66
Gluten-free bread	90
Hamburger bun	61
Kaiser roll	73
Melba toast	70
Oat kernel (80% kernels)	65
Oat bran (two studies)	47
Pumpernickel (whole-grain)	51
Rye kernel (six studies)	50
Rye flour (ten studies)	65
Sourdough	52
Wheat (white flour, five studies)	70

Food Tested	Glycemic Index Mean (Glucose = 100)
Wheat (whole-meal flour, twelve studies)	69
Pita, white	57
Semolina	64
Bulgur (three studies)	52
Mixed grain (four studies)	45
Breakfast Cereals	
All-Bran (four studies)	42
Bran Buds with Psyllium (Kellogg's)	45
Bran Chex	58
Bran Flakes (Post)	74
Cheerios	74
Cocopops	77
Corn bran	75
Corn Chex	83
Cornflakes (four studies)	84
Cream of Wheat, Instant	74
Crispix	87
Grape Nuts	67
Grape Nuts Flakes	80
Muesli, toasted	43
Oat bran, raw (two studies)	55
Oatmeal (made with water, cooked)	49
Porridge, including quick oats (eight studies)	61
Puffed wheat (two studies)	74
Rice bran	19
Rice Chex	89
Rice Krispies (Kellogg's)	82
Shredded Wheat (three studies)	69

Food Tested	Glycemic Index Mean (Glucose = 100)
Breakfast Cereals *(continued)*	
Special K	54
Total	76
Cereal Grains	
Barley (four studies)	25
Buckwheat (three studies)	54
Bulgur (four studies)	48
Couscous (two studies)	65
Maize cornmeal	68
Millet	71
Rice, brown (three studies)	55
Rice, instant (two studies)	91
Rice, parboiled (thirteen studies)	47
Rice, white, high-amylose (three studies)	59
Rice, white, low-amylose (three studies)	88
Rice, white (thirteen studies)	56
Rye, whole kernel (three studies)	34
Sweet corn (seven studies)	55
Wheat, whole kernel (four studies)	41
Cookies	
Graham wafers	74
Oatmeal	55
Shortbread	64
Vanilla wafers	77
Crackers	
Rice cakes	82
Rye crispbread, high-fiber (five studies)	65

Food Tested	Glycemic Index Mean (Glucose = 100)
Wheat Thins	67
Water crackers	72
Dairy	
Ice cream (five studies)	61
Ice cream, low-fat	50
Milk, chocolate, with sugar	34
Milk, full-fat (four studies)	27
Milk, skim	32
Tofu frozen dessert, nondairy	115
Yogurt, low-fat, fruit, with sugar	33
Fruit	
Apple (four studies)	36
Apple juice, unsweetened (two studies)	41
Apricots, canned, light syrup	64
Apricots, dried (two studies)	31
Banana (six studies)	53
Cherries	22
Dates, dried	103
Fruit cocktail, canned	55
Grapefruit	25
Grapefruit juice, unsweetened	48
Grapes	43
Kiwifruit (two studies)	52
Mango (two studies)	55
Orange (four studies)	43
Orange juice (four studies)	57
Papaya (two studies)	58
Peach	28

Food Tested	Glycemic Index Mean (Glucose = 100)
Fruit *(continued)*	
Peach, canned, natural juice	30
Peach, canned, light syrup	52
Peach, canned, heavy syrup	58
Pear (three studies)	36
Pear, canned, natural juice	44
Pineapple	66
Pineapple juice, unsweetened	46
Plum	24
Raisins	64
Watermelon	72
Legumes, Vegetables	
Baked beans, canned (two studies)	48
Beets	64
Black beans, boiled	30
Black-eyed peas (two studies)	42
Butter beans (three studies)	31
Chickpeas (three studies)	33
Chickpeas, canned	42
Kidney beans (seven studies)	27
Kidney beans, canned	52
Lentils, green (three studies)	30
Lentils, green, canned	52
Lentils, red (four studies)	26
Lima beans, baby, frozen	32
Navy beans (five studies)	38
Peas, dried	22
Peas, green (three studies)	48
Pinto beans	39

Food Tested	Glycemic Index Mean (Glucose = 100)
Pinto beans, canned	45
Pumpkin	75
Soya beans (two studies)	18
Soya beans, canned	14
Vegetables	
Carrots (two studies)	71
French fries	75
Parsnips	97
Potato, baked (four studies)	85
Potato, instant (five studies)	83
Potato, new (three studies)	62
Potato, white, boiled (three studies)	56
Potato, white, mashed (three studies)	70
Potato, white, steamed	65
Sweet corn (seven studies)	55
Sweet potato (two studies)	54
Rutabaga	72
Yam	51
Pasta	
Capellini	45
Fettucini, egg-enriched	32
Linguini, thick, durum (two studies)	46
Linguini, thin, durum (two studies)	55
Macaroni, boiled five minutes	45
Macaroni and cheese, boxed	64
Ravioli, durum, meat-filled	39
Spaghetti, durum (three studies)	55
Spaghetti, white (ten studies)	41

Food Tested	Glycemic Index Mean (Glucose = 100)
Pasta *(continued)*	
Spaghetti, whole-meal (two studies)	37
Vermicelli	35
Snacks and Candy	
Chocolate	49
Coca-Cola, one can	63
Corn chips (two studies)	73
Jelly beans	80
Life Savers	70
Mars Bar	68
Muesli bar	61
Peanuts (three studies)	14
Popcorn	55
Soups	
Black bean	64
Green pea, canned	66
Lentil, canned	44
Tomato	38
Sugars	
Fructose (four studies)	23
Glucose (eight studies)	97
Honey (two studies)	73
Maltose	105
Sucrose (six studies)	65
Lactose (two studies)	46

Food Tested	Glycemic Index Mean (Glucose = 100)
Ethnic Foods	
Breadfruit	68
Corn hominy	40
Maize meal porridge, unrefined	71
Nopal, prickly pear cactus	7
Rice vermicelli	58
Tapioca, steamed one hour	70
Taro	54

Source: Data from K. Foster-Powell and J. Miller, "International Tables of Glycemic Index," *American Journal of Clinical Nutrition* 62, no. 4 (1995): 871S-893S, and J. Brand-Miller, T. Wolever, S. Colagiuri, and K. Foster-Powell, *The Glucose Revolution: The Authoritative Guide to the Glycemic Index—The Groundbreaking Medical Discovery* (New York: Marlowe & Company, 1999).

Note: Food types that were assessed in multiple studies were assigned a glycemic index representing the mathematical mean of those studies.

APPENDIX II

RESOURCES

SUGGESTED READINGS

Huggins, Hal. *It's All in Your Head: The Link Between Mercury Amalgams and Illness.* Garden City Park, N.Y.: Avery Publishing Group, Inc., 1993.

Huggins, Hal, and Thomas Levy. *Uninformed Consent: The Hidden Dangers in Dental Care.* Charlottesville, Va.: Hampton Roads Publishing Company, Inc., 1999.

Meinig, George. *Root Canal Cover-Up.* Ojai, Calif.: Bion Publishing, 1996.

Page, Melvin E., and H. Leon Abrams. *Your Body Is Your Best Doctor.* New Canaan, Conn.: Keats Publishing, Inc., 1972.

Price, Weston. *Nutrition and Physical Degeneration.* New Canaan, Conn.: Keats Publishing, Inc., 1989.

FOR FURTHER EDUCATION AND ASSISTANCE

1. Regarding dental toxicity and help with attaining a Total Dental Revision:

   Hal A. Huggins, D.D.S., M.S.
   Office: (719) 522-0566
   Toll-free: 1-866-948-4638 (9HUGNET)
   Fax: (719) 548-8220
   Web site: www.hugnet.com

   Thomas E. Levy, M.D., J.D.
   Office: (719) 548-1600
   Toll-free: 1-800-331-2303
   Fax: (719) 572-8081
   E-mail: televy@medmail.com
   Web site: www.peakenergy.com

2. Serum biocompatibility testing for replacement dental materials:

   Peak Energy Performance, Inc.
   Contact Dr. Levy for information.

3. Nutrition books and related information:

   Price-Pottenger Nutrition Foundation
   P.O. Box 2614
   La Mesa, CA 91943-2614
   Office: (619) 574-PPNF
   Toll-free: 1-800-366-3748
   Fax: (619) 574-1314
   E-mail: info@price-pottenger.org

4. Bioavailable supplements (designed by Dr. Huggins) and information on dental toxicity:

   Contact Dr. Huggins for information.

5. To order vitamin C as sodium ascorbate powder:

   Bronson Laboratories
   600 E. Quality Drive
   American Fork, Utah 84003
   Toll-free: 1-800-235-3200

6. For more information on the safe use of biomagnetism, magnetic water softening, and many other practical applications of magnetism:

   Magnetizer
   5525 Swamp Road
   Fountainville, PA 18923-9612
   Office: (215) 249-1200
   Fax: (215) 249-3161
   E-mail: mgimag@magnetizer.com

NOTES

Chapter 1

1. Lavers, M., S. Saint-Hillaire, and C. Code. "Gastric Secretory Equivalent of Different Foods." *Physiologist* 1, no. 4 (1958): 47.

Chapter 2

1. Dries, Jan, and Inge Dries. *The Complete Book of Food Combining: A New Approach to the Hay Diet and Healthy Eating.* Rockport, Mass.: Element Books, Inc., 1998.

2. Phillips, R. "Role of Life-style and Dietary Habits Among Seventh-Day Adventists." *Cancer Research* 35, no. 11 (Pt. 2) (1975): 3513–3522.

3. Willett, W., et al. "Relation of Meat, Fat, and Fiber Intake to the Risk of Colon Cancer in a Prospective Study Among Women." *The New England Journal of Medicine* 323, no. 24 (1990): 1664–1667.

4. Slattery, M., et al. "Eating Patterns and Risk of Colon Cancer." *American Journal of Epidemiology* 148, no. 1 (1998): 4–16.

5. Grant, Doris, and Jean Joice. *Food Combining for Health: Get Fit with Foods That Don't Fight.* Rochester, Vt.: Healing Arts Press, 1989.

6. Maier, B., et al. "Effects of a High-beef Diet on Bowel-flora: A Preliminary Report." *The American Journal of Clinical Nutrition* 27 (1974): 1470–1474.

7. Billing, J., and P. Sherman. "Antimicrobial Functions of Spices: Why Some Like It Hot." *Quarterly Review of Biology* 73, no. 1 (March 1998): 3–49.

8. Ceylan, E., D. Kang, and Y. Fung. "Reduction of *Escherichia coli* O157:H7 in Ground Meat by Selected Spices." Presentation, Institute of Food Technologists' 1998 Annual Meeting & Food Expo.

9. Gay, D., R. Cox, and J. Reinhardt. "Chewing Releases Mercury from Fillings." *Lancet* 1 (1979): 985–986.

10. Svare, C., et al. "The Effect of Dental Amalgams on Mercury Levels in Expired Air." *Journal of Dental Research* 60, no. 9 (1981): 1668–1671.

11. Summers, A., et al. "Mercury Released from Dental 'Silver' Fillings Provokes an Increase in Mercury- and Antibiotic-resistant Bacteria in Oral and Intestinal Floras of Primates." *Antimicrobial Agents and Chemotherapy* 37, no. 4 (1993): 825–834.

CHAPTER 3

1. Pyorala, M., et al. "Hyperinsulinemia Predicts Coronary Heart Disease Risk in Healthy Middle-aged Men: The 22-Year Follow-up Results of the Helsinki Policemen Study." *Circulation* 98, no. 5 (1998): 398–404.

2. Saito, T., Y. Shimazaki, and M. Sakamoto. "Obesity and Periodontitis." *New England Journal of Medicine* 339, no. 7 (1998): 482–483.

3. Page, Melvin E., and H. Leon Abrams. *Your Body Is Your Best Doctor.* New Canaan, Conn.: Keats Publishing, Inc., 1972.

4. Shoff, S., and P. Newcomb. "Diabetes, Body Size, and Risk of Endometrial Cancer." *American Journal of Epidemiology* 148, no. 3 (1998): 234–240.

5. Price, Weston. *Nutrition and Physical Degeneration.* New Canaan, Conn.: Keats Publishing, Inc., 1989.

6. Wilson, A., et al. "Relation of Infant Diet to Childhood Health: Seven-Year Follow-Up of Cohort of Children in Dundee Infant Feeding Study." *BMJ (Clinical Research Ed.)* 316, no. 7124 (1998): 21–25.

7. Winkleby, M., et al. "Ethnic and Socioeconomic Differences in Cardiovascular Disease Risk Factors: Findings for Women from the Third National Health and Nutrition Examination Survey, 1988–1994." *Journal of the American Medical Association* 280, no. 4 (1998): 356–362.

8. Schenck, C., and M. Mahowald. "Review of Nocturnal Sleep-related Eating Disorders." *International Journal of Eating Disorders* 15, no. 4 (1994): 343–356.

9. Knowler W., et al. "Diabetes Mellitus in the Pima Indians: Incidence, Risk Factors and Pathogenesis." *Diabetes and Metabolism Review* 6, no. 1 (1990): 1–27.

10. Fernandes, O., et al. "Moderate to Heavy Caffeine Consumption During Pregnancy and Relationship to Spontaneous Abortion and Abnormal Fetal Growth: A Meta-analysis." *Reproductive Toxicology* 12, no. 4 (1998): 435–444.

CHAPTER 4

1. Seely, S. "Diet and Coronary Disease: A Survey of Mortality Rates and Food Consumption Statistics of 24 Countries." *Medical Hypotheses* 7, no. 7 (1981): 907–918.

2. Seely, S. "Diet and Coronary Disease: A Survey of Female Mortality Rates and Food Consumption Statistics of 21 Countries." *Medical Hypotheses* 7, no. 9 (1981): 1133–1137.

3. Seely, S. "Diet and Coronary Arterial Disease: A Statistical Study." *International Journal of Cardiology* 20, no. 2 (1988): 183–192.

4. Pottenger, E., and R. Pottenger, eds. *Pottenger's Cats: A Study in Nutrition.* La Mesa, Calif.: The Price-Pottenger Nutrition Foundation (The edited writings of Dr. Francis Pottenger), 1983.

5. Otto, C., et al. "Association of Aortic-valve Sclerosis with Cardiovascular Mortality and Morbidity in the Elderly." *New England Journal of Medicine* 341, no. 3 (1999): 142–147.

6. Doherty, T., et al. "Coronary Calcium: The Good, the Bad, and the Uncertain." *American Heart Journal* 137, no. 5 (1999): 806–814.

7. Samaras, T., and G. Heigh. "How Human Size Affects Longevity and Mortality from Degenerative Diseases." *Townsend Letter for Doctors & Patients* (October 1996): 78–85, 133–139.

8. Page, Melvin E., and H. Leon Abrams. *Your Body Is Your Best Doctor.* New Canaan, Conn.: Keats Publishing, Inc., 1972.

9. Juskevich, J., and G. Guyer. "Bovine Growth Hormone: Human Food Safety Evaluation." *Science* 249, no. 4971 (1990): 875–884.

10. Cohen, Robert. *Milk: The Deadly Poison.* Englewood Cliffs, N.J.: Argus Publishing, Inc., 1998.

CHAPTER 5

1. Golomb, B. "Cholesterol and Violence: Is There a Connection?" *Annals of Internal Medicine* 128, no. 6 (1998): 478–487.

2. Lazarou, J., B. Pomeranz, and P. Corey. "Incidence of Adverse Drug Reactions in Hospitalized Patients: A Meta-analysis of Prospective Studies." *Journal of the American Medical Association* 279, no. 15 (1998): 1200–1205.

3. Shih, D., et al. "Mice Lacking Serum Paraoxonase Are Susceptible to Organophosphate Toxicity and Atherosclerosis." *Nature* 394, no. 6690 (1998): 284–287.

4. John, S., et al. "Increased Bioavailabity of Nitric Oxide after Lipid-lowering Therapy in Hypercholesterolemic Patients: A Randomized, Placebo-controlled, Double-blind Study." *Circulation* 98, no. 3 (1998): 211–216.

5. Ridker, P., et al. "Long-term Effects of Pravastatin on Plasma Concentration on C-reactive Protein. The Cholesterol and Recurrent Events (CARE) Investigators." *Circulation* 100, no. 3 (1999): 230–235.

6. Ross, S., et al. "Clinical Outcomes in Statin Treatment Trials: A Meta-analysis." *Archives of Internal Medicine* 159, no. 15 (1999): 1793–1802.

7. Alouf, J. "Les Toxines Cytolytiques Bacteriennes Thiol-dependantes: Streptolysine O et Toxines Apparentées" (Thiol-dependent Cytolytic Bacterial Toxins: Streptolysin O and Prominent Toxins). *Archives de l'Institut Pasteur de Tunis* 58, no. 3 (1981): 355–373.

8. Chi, M., et al. "Effect of T-2 Toxin on Brain Catecholamines and Selected Blood Components in Growing Chickens." *Poultry Science* 60, no. 1 (1981): 137–141.

9. Watson, K., and E. Kerr. "Functional Role of Cholesterol in Infection and Autoimmunity." *Lancet* 1, no. 7902 (1975): 308–310.

10. Kossman, S., J. Wysocki, and J. Nawrot. "Lipoproteiny Surowicy Krwi u Pracownikowbrygad Remontowych Zakladow Chemicznych 'Organika-Azot' w Jaworznie" (Blood Serum Lipoproteins in Overhaul Workers of the Chemical Plant at Jaworzno). *Medycyna Pracy* 44, no. 2 (1993): 103–108.

11. Bloomer, A., et al. "A Study of Pesticide Residues in Michigan's General Population, 1968–70." *Pesticides Monitoring Journal* 11, no. 3 (1977): 111–115.

12. Davies, T., S. Nielsen, and B. Jortner. "Pathology of Chronic and Subacute Canine Methylmercurialism." *Journal of the American Animal Hospital Association* 13, no. 3 (1977): 369–381.

13. Schatzkin, A., et al. "Serum Cholesterol and Cancer in the NHANES I Epidemiologic Follow-up Study. National Health and Nutrition Examination Study." *Lancet* 2, no. 8554 (1987): 298–301.

14. Cowan, L., et al. "Cancer Mortality and Lipid and Lipoprotein Levels. Lipid Research Clinics Program Mortality Follow-up Study." *American Journal of Epidemiology* 131, no. 3 (1990): 468–482.

15. Davis, C., et al. "Serum Cholesterol Levels and Cancer Mortality: Evans County Twenty-year Follow-up Study." *American Oil Chemists Society* (1982): 892–900.

16. Keys, A., et al. "Serum Cholesterol and Cancer Mortality in the Seven Countries Study." *American Journal of Epidemiology* 121, no. 6 (1985): 870–883.

17. Gerhardsson, M., et al. "Serum Cholesterol and Cancer—A Retrospective Case-control Study." *International Journal of Epidemiology* 15, no. 2 (1986): 155–159.

18. Isles, C., et al. "Plasma Cholesterol, Coronary Heart Disease, and Cancer in the Renfrew and Paisley Survey." *BMJ (Clinical Research Ed.)* 298, no. 6678 (1989): 920–924.

19. Kagan, A., et al. "Serum Cholesterol and Mortality in a Japanese-American Population: The Honolulu Heart Program." *American Journal of Epidemiology* 114, no. 1 (1981): 11–20.

20. Knekt, P., et al. "Serum Cholesterol and Risk of Cancer in a Cohort of 39,000 Men and Women." *Journal of Clinical Epidemiology* 41 (1988): 519–530.

21. Kark, J., A. Smith, and C. Hames. "The Relationship of Serum Cholesterol to the Incidence of Cancer in Evans County, Georgia." *Journal of Chronic Diseases* 33 (1980): 311–332.

22. Stemmermann, G., et al. "Serum Cholesterol and Colon Cancer Incidence in Hawaiian Japanese Men." *Journal of the National Cancer Institute* 67, no. 6 (1981): 1179–1182.

23. Williams, R., et al. "Cancer Incidence by Levels of Cholesterol." *Journal of the American Medical Association* 245, no. 3 (1981): 247–252.

24. Simon, J., and E. Hudes. "Serum Ascorbic Acid and Other Correlates of Gallbladder Disease Among U.S. Adults." *American Journal of Public Health* 88, no. 8 (1998): 1208–1212.

25. Haley, R. "Point: Bias from the 'Healthy-warrior Effect' and Unequal Follow-up in Three Government Studies of Health Effects of the Gulf War." *American Journal of Epidemiology* 148, no. 4 (1998): 315–323.

26. Eastwood, M., and M. Trevelyan. "Relationship Between Physical and Psychiatric Disorder." *Psychological Medicine* 2, no. 4 (1972): 363–372.

27. Ford, D., et al. "Depression Is a Risk Factor for Coronary Artery Disease in Men: The Precursors Study." *Archives of Internal Medicine* 158, no. 13 (1998): 1422–1426.

28. Barefoot, A., and M. Schroll. "Symptoms of Depression, Acute Myocardial Infarction, and Total Mortality in a Community Sample." *Circulation* 93, no. 11 (1996): 1976–1980.

29. von Ammon Cavanaugh, S., et al. "Medical Illness, Past Depression, and Present Depression: A Predictive Triad for In-hospital Mortality." *American Journal of Psychiatry* 158, no. 1 (2001): 43–48.

30. Neeleman, J., S. Wessely, and M. Wadsworth. "Predictors of Suicide, Accidental Death, and Premature Natural Death in a General-population Birth Cohort." *Lancet* 351, no. 9096 (1998): 93–97.

31. Price, Weston. *Nutrition and Physical Degeneration.* New Canaan, Conn.: Keats Publishing, Inc., 1989.

CHAPTER 6

1. Bakir, F., et al. "Methylmercury Poisoning in Iraq." *Science* 181, no. 96 (1973): 230–241.

2. Ballatori, N., M. Lieberman, and W. Wong. "N-acetylcysteine as an Antidote in Methylmercury Poisoning." *Environmental Health Perspectives* 106, no. 5 (1998): 267–271.

3. Ornaghi, F., et al. "The Protective Effects of N-acetyl-L-cysteine Against Methyl Mercury Embryotoxicity in Mice." *Fundamental and Applied Toxicology: Official Journal of the Society of Toxicology* 20, no. 4 (1993): 437–445.

4. Hagmar, L., et al. "Plasma Levels of Selenium, Selenoprotein P and Glutathione Peroxidase and Their Correlations to Fish Intake and Serum Levels of Thyrotropin and Thyroid Hormones: A Study on Latvian Fish Consumers." *European Journal of Clinical Nutrition* 52, no. 11 (1998): 796–800.

5. Drexler, H., and K. Schaller. "The Mercury Concentration in Breast Milk Resulting from Amalgam Fillings and Dietary Habits." *Environmental Research* 77, no. 2 (1998): 124–129.

CHAPTER 7

1. Crystal, S., and I. Bernstein. "Infant Salt Preference and Mother's Morning Sickness." *Appetite* 30, no. 3 (1998): 297–307.

2. Yiamouyiannis, John. *Fluoride: The Aging Factor.* Delaware, Ohio: Health Action Press, 1993.

3. Yiamouyiannis, J., and D. Burk. "Fluoridation and Cancer: Age Dependence of Cancer Mortality Related to Artificial Fluoridation." *Fluoride* 10, no. 3 (1977): 102–123.

4. Price, Joseph M. *Coronaries/Cholesterol/Chlorine.* New York: Jove Books, The Berkley Publishing Group, 1969.

CHAPTER 8

1. Zhang, Y., et al. "Bone Mass and the Risk of Breast Cancer Among Postmenopausal Women." *The New England Journal of Medicine* 336, no. 9 (1997): 611–617.

2. Lucas, F., et al. "Bone Mineral Density and Risk of Breast Cancer: Differences by Family History of Breast Cancer. Study of Osteoporotic Fractures Research Group." *American Journal of Epidemiology* 148, no. 1 (1998): 22–29.

3. Cauley, J., et al. "Bone Mineral Density and Risk of Breast Cancer in Older Women: The Study of Osteoporotic Fractures. Study of Osteoporotic Fractures Research Group." *Journal of the American Medical Association* 276, no. 17 (1996): 1404–1408.

4. Evans, A., et al. "Mammographic Features of Ductal Carcinoma in Situ (DCIS) Present on Previous Mammography." *Clinical Radiology* 54, no. 10 (1999): 644–646.

5. Curhan, G., et al. "Comparison of Dietary Calcium with Supplemental Calcium and Other Nutrients as Factors Affecting the Risk for Kidney Stones in Women." *Annals of Internal Medicine* 126, no. 7 (1997): 497–504.

6. Melhus, H., et al. "Excessive Dietary Intake of Vitamin A Is Associated with Reduced Bone Mineral Density and Increased Risk for Hip Fracture." *Annals of Internal Medicine* 129, no. 10 (1998): 770–778.

7. Schwartzman, M., and W. Franck. "Vitamin D Toxicity Complicating the Treatment of Senile, Postmenopausal, and Glucocorticoid-induced Osteoporosis. Four Case Reports and a Critical Commentary on the Use of Vitamin D in These Disorders." *American Journal of Medicine* 82, no. 2 (1987): 224–230.

8. Rapola, J., et al. "Randomised Trial of Alpha-tocopherol and Beta-carotene Supplements on Incidence of Major Coronary Events in Men with Previous Myocardial Infarction." *Lancet* 349, no. 9067 (1997): 1715–1720.

9. Jumaan, A., et al. "Beta-carotene Intake and Risk of Postmenopausal Breast Cancer." *Epidemiology* 10, no. 1 (1999): 49–53.

10. Kurtz, T., H. Al-Bander, and R. Morris. " 'Salt-sensitive' Essential Hypertension in Men. Is the Sodium Ion Alone Important?" *The New England Journal of Medicine* 317, no. 17 (1987): 1043–1048.

11. Kurtz, T., and R. Morris. "Dietary Chloride as a Determinant of 'Sodium-dependent' Hypertension." *Science* 222, no. 4628 (1983): 1139–1141.

12. Klenner, F. R. "Massive Doses of Vitamin C and the Virus Diseases." *Southern Medicine & Surgery* 103, no. 4 (April 1951): 101–107.

13. Klenner, F. R. "The Use of Vitamin C as an Antibiotic." *Journal of Applied Nutrition* 6, (1953): 274–278.

14. Klenner, F. R. "Observations on the Dose and Administration of Ascorbic Acid When Employed Beyond the Range of a Vitamin in Human Pathology." *Journal of Applied Nutrition* 23, nos. 3–4 (Winter 1971): 61–88.

15. Klenner, F. R. "Significance of High Daily Intake of Ascorbic Acid in Preventive Medicine." *Journal of the International Academy of Preventive Medicine* 1, no. 1 (Spring 1974): 45–69.

16. Cathcart, R. "The Method of Determining Proper Doses of Vitamin C for the Treatment of Disease by Titrating to Bowel Tolerance." *The Journal of Orthomolecular Psychiatry* 10, no. 2 (1981): 125–132.

17. Womble, D., and J. Helderman. "Enhancement of Allo-responsiveness of Human Lymphocytes by Acemannan (Carrisyn)." *International Journal of Immunopharmacology* 10, no. 8 (1988): 967–974.

18. Womble, D., and J. Helderman. "The Impact of Acemannan on the Generation and Function of Cytotoxic T-lymphocytes." *Immunopharmacology and Immunotoxicology* 14, nos. 1–2 (1992): 63–77.

19. Zhang, L., and I. Tizard. "Activation of a Mouse Macrophage Cell Line by Acemannan: The Major Carbohydrate Fraction from Aloe Vera Gel." *Immunopharmacology* 35, no. 2 (1996): 119–128.

20. Langsjoen, P., et al. "Pronounced Increase of Survival of Patients with Cardiomyopathy when Treated with Coenzyme Q10 and Conventional Therapy." *International Journal of Tissue Reactions* 12, no. 3 (1990): 163–168.

21. Lockwood, K., et al. "Progress on Therapy of Breast Cancer with Coenzyme Q10 and the Regression of Metastases." *Biochemical and Biophysical Research Communications* 212, no. 1 (1995): 172–177.

22. Folkers, K., M. Morita, and J. McRee. "The Activities of Coenzyme Q10 and Vitamin B_6 for Immune Responses." *Biochemical and Biophysical Research Communications* 193, no. 1 (1993): 88–92.

23. Angele, M., et al. "Dehydroepiandrosterone: An Inexpensive Steroid Hormone that Decreases the Mortality Due to Sepsis Following Trauma-induced Hemorrhage." *Archives of Surgery* 133, no. 12 (1998): 1281–1288.

24. Ommen, S., et al. "Predictive Power of the Relative Lymphocyte Concentration in Patients with Advanced Heart Failure." *Circulation* 97, no. 1 (1998): 19–22.

CHAPTER 9

1. Eggleston, D., and M. Nylander. "Correlation of Dental Amalgam with Mercury in Brain Tissues." *Journal of Prosthetic Dentistry* 58, no. 6 (1987): 704–707.

2. Sunderman, F. "Mechanisms of Nickel Carcinogenesis." *Scandinavian Journal of Work, Environment & Health* 15, no. 1 (1989): 1–12.

3. Scannapieco, F., and R. Genco. "Association of Periodontal Infections with Atherosclerotic and Pulmonary Diseases." *Journal of Periodontal Research* 34, no. 7 (1999): 340–345.

4. Beck, James, et al. "Periodontal Disease and Cardiovascular Disease." *Journal of Periodontology* 67, no. 10 (suppl) (1996): 1123–1137.

5. Levy, T., and H. Huggins. "Routine Dental Extractions Routinely Produce Cavitations." *Journal of Advancement in Medicine* 9, no. 4 (1996): 235–249.

6. Joshipura, K., C. Douglass, and W. Willett. "Possible Explanations for the Tooth Loss and Cardiovascular Disease Relationship." *Annals of Periodontology* 3, no. 1 (1998): 175–183.

7. Coogan, C., et al. "Bilateral Testicular Tumors: Management and Outcome in Twenty-one Patients." *Cancer* 83, no. 3 (1998): 547–552.

8. Trappier, A., P. Lorio, and L. Johnson. "Evolving Perspectives on the Exposure Risks from Magnetic Fields." *Journal of the National Medical Association* 82, no. 9 (1990): 621–624.

9. Davis, Albert R., and Walter Rawls. *Magnetism and Its Effects on the Living System.* Kansas City, Mo.: Acres U.S.A., 1974.

10. Davis, Albert R., and Walter Rawls. *The Magnetic Effect.* Kansas City, Mo.: Acres U.S.A., 1975.

11. Davis, Albert R., and Walter Rawls. *The Rainbow in Your Hands.* Kansas City, Mo.: Acres U.S.A., 1976.

12. Davis, Albert R., and Walter Rawls. *The Magnetic Blueprint of Life.* Kansas City, Mo.: Acres U.S.A., 1979.

CHAPTER 10

1. Huggins, Hal, and Thomas Levy. *Uninformed Consent: The Hidden Dangers in Dental Care.* Charlottesville, Va.: Hampton Roads Publishing Company, Inc., 1999.

2. Huggins, Hal. *It's All in Your Head: The Link Between Mercury Amalgams and Illness.* Garden City Park, N.Y.: Avery Publishing Group, Inc., 1993.

BIBLIOGRAPHY

Batmanghelidj, F. *Your Body's Many Cries for Water: Don't Treat Thirst with Medications.* Falls Church, Va.: Global Health Solutions, Inc., 1992.

Bennett, J., and F. Plum, eds. *Cecil Textbook of Medicine.* Philadelphia, Pa.: W.B. Saunders Company, 1996.

Brown, R. *Bee Hive Product Bible.* Garden City Park, N.Y.: Avery Publishing Group, Inc., 1993.

Burtis, C., and E. Ashwood, eds. *Tietz Textbook of Clinical Chemistry.* 2d ed. Philadelphia, Pa.: W.B. Saunders Company, 1994.

Carlson, L., et al. "Reduction of Myocardial Reinfarction by the Combined Treatment with Clofibrate and Nicotinic Acid." *Atherosclerosis* 28, no. 1 (1977): 81–86.

Committee of Principal Investigators. "A Co-operative Trial in the Primary Prevention of Ischaemic Heart Disease Using Clofibrate." *British Heart Journal* 40, no. 10 (1978): 1069–1118.

Coronary Drug Project Research Group. "Clofibrate and Niacin in Coronary Heart Disease." *Journal of the American Medical Association* 231, no. 4 (1975): 360–381.

Diamond, Harvey, and Marilyn Diamond. *Fit for Life.* New York: Warner Books, Inc., 1985.

———. *Fit for Life II: Living Health.* New York: Warner Books, Inc., 1987.

Dimai, H., et al. "Daily Oral Magnesium Supplementation Suppresses Bone Turnover in Young Adult Males." *Journal of Endocrinology and Metabolism* 83, no. 8 (1998): 2742–2748.

Dorland's Illustrated Medical Dictionary. Philadelphia, Pa.: W.B. Saunders Company, 1994.

Dorr, A., et al. "Colestipol Hydrochloride in Hypercholesterolemic Patients—Effect on Serum Cholesterol and Mortality." *Journal of Chronic Diseases* 31, no. 1 (1978): 5–14.

Douglass, William C. *Eat Your Cholesterol: How to Live Off the Fat of the Land and Feel Great!* Atlanta, Ga.: Second Opinion Publishing, 1993.

———. *The Milk Book: How Science Is Destroying Nature's Nearly Perfect Food.* Dunwoody, Ga.: Second Opinion Publishing, 1993.

Erasmus, Udo. *Fats That Heal, Fats That Kill.* Burnaby B.C. Canada: Alive Books, 1993.

Fallon, Sally, and Mary G. Enig. "Soy Products for Dairy Products? Not So Fast." *Health Freedom News,* September 1995.

Finnegan, John. *The Facts About Fats: A Consumer's Guide to Good Oils.* Malibu, Calif.: Elysian Arts, 1992.

Frick, M., et al. "Helsinki Heart Study: Primary-Prevention Trial with Gemfibrozil in Middle-aged Men with Dyslipidemia.

Safety of Treatment, Changes in Risk Factors, and Incidence of Coronary Heart Disease." *New England Journal of Medicine* 317, no. 20 (1987): 1237–1245.

Ganther, H. "Interactions of Vitamin E and Selenium with Mercury and Silver." *Annals of the New York Academy of Sciences* 355 (1980): 212–216.

Graves, J. "Hyperkalemia Due to a Potassium-based Water Softener." *New England Journal of Medicine* 339, no. 24 (1998): 1790–1791.

Groff, J., S. Gropper, and S. Hunt. *Advanced Nutrition and Human Metabolism.* St. Paul, Minn.: West Publishing Company, 1995.

Guyton, Arthur C., and John E. Hall. *Textbook of Medical Physiology.* Philadelphia, Pa.: W.B. Saunders Company, 1996.

Haffner, S., et al. "Mortality from Coronary Heart Disease in Subjects with Type 2 Diabetes and in Nondiabetic Subjects with and without Prior Myocardial Infarction." *New England Journal of Medicine* 339, no. 4 (1998): 229–234.

Jensen, Bernard, and S. Bell. *Tissue Cleansing Through Bowel Management.* Escondido, Calif.: Bernard Jensen, D.C., Ph.D., 1981.

Kulish, Peter. *Conquering Pain: The Art of Healing with Biomagnetism.* Fountainville, Penn.: Fountainville Press, 1999.

Larsson, M., et al. "Improved Zinc and Iron Absorption from Breakfast Meals Containing Malted Oats with Reduced Phytate Content." *British Journal of Nutrition* 76, no. 5 (1996): 677–688.

Lehmann, C. *Saunders Manual of Clinical Laboratory Science.* Philadelphia, Pa.: W.B. Saunders Company, 1998.

Lyon J., et al. "Low Cancer Incidence and Mortality in Utah." *Cancer* 39, no. 6 (1977): 2608–2618.

Meinig, George. *Root Canal Cover-up.* Ojai, Calif.: Bion Publishing, 1996.

Miki, H., et al. "Inhibition of Intercellular Communication by Nickel(II): Antagonistic Effect of Magnesium." *Carcinogenesis* 8, no. 11 (1987): 1757–1760.

Nasset, E. "Physiology of the Digestive System." In *Medical Physiology,* vol. I, 12th ed., edited by V. Mountcasle. St. Louis, Mo.: The C.V. Mosby Company, 1968.

Physicians' Desk Reference. Montvale, N.J.: Medical Economics Company, 50th ed., 1996.

Queen, H. *Chronic Mercury Toxicity: New Hope Against an Endemic Disease.* Colorado Springs, Colo.: Queen and Company Health Communications, Inc., 1988.

Rand, C., A. Macgregor, and A. Stunkard. "The Night Eating Syndrome in the General Population and Among Postoperative Obesity Surgery Patients." *International Journal of Eating Disorders* 22, no. 1 (1997): 65–69.

Schmid, R. *Traditional Foods Are Your Best Medicine: Improving Health and Longevity with Native Nutrition.* Rochester, Vt.: Healing Arts Press, 1997.

Shapiro, R., C. Hatheway, and D. Swerdlow. "Botulism in the United States: A Clinical and Epidemiologic Review." *Annals of Internal Medicine* 129, no. 3 (1998): 221–228.

Simone, C. *Cancer and Nutrition: A Ten-Point Plan to Reduce Your Risk of Getting Cancer.* Garden City Park, N.Y.: Avery Publishing Group, Inc., 1992.

Smith, Lendon. *The Clinical Experiences of Frederick R. Klenner, M.D.: Clinical Guide to the Use of Vitamin C.* Life Sciences Press, 1988.

Steward, H. Leighton, et al. *Sugar Busters! Cut Sugar to Trim Fat.* New York: The Ballantine Publishing Group, 1998.

Taylor, P., and D. Albanes. "Selenium, Vitamin E, and Prostate Cancer—Ready for Prime Time?" *Journal of the National Cancer Institute* 90, no. 16 (1998): 1184–1185.

Wade, Carlson. *Fact/Book on Fats, Oils, and Cholesterol.* New Canaan, Conn.: Keats Publishing, Inc., 1973.

The Webster Reference Dictionary of the English Language. Encyclopedic edition. Delair Publishing Company, Inc., 1983.

Whitescarver, S., et al. "Salt-sensitive Hypertension: Contribution of Chloride." *Science* 223, no. 4643 (1984): 1430–1432.

Zeromski, J., et al. "The Effect of Nickel Compounds on Immunophenotype and Natural Killer Cell Function of Normal Human Lymphocytes." *Toxicology* 97, no. 1–3 (1995): 39–48.

Zhou, J., et al. "Reduction of Phytic Acid in Soybean Products Improves Zinc Bioavailability in Rats." *Journal of Nutrition* 122, no. 2 (1992): 2466–2473.

INDEX